# TEACHER'S PET PUBLICATIONS

LITPLAN TEACHER PACK
for
Fahrenheit 451
based on the book by
Ray Bradbury

Written by
Mary B. Collins

ISBN 978-1-60249-160-1

This **LitPlan** for Ray Bradbury's
Fahrenheit 451
has been brought to you by Teacher's Pet Publications, Inc.

Copyright Teacher's Pet Publications 1996

www.tpet.com

TABLE OF CONTENTS - *Fahrenheit 451*

A FEW NOTES ABOUT THE AUTHOR
RAY BRADBURY

Ray Bradbury was born on August 22, 1920 in Wankegan, Illinois, but he grew up in Los Angeles, California. At an early age he learned to disregard criticism of his likes and dislikes and to do what made him happy. Film also played an important role in his formative years. By the time he got to high school, he was writing short stories, leading up to the sale of his first story on his twenty-first birthday.

Some of Mr. Bradbrury's most well-known works include *The Martian Chronicles* (1950), *Fahrenheit 451* (1953), *Something Wicked This Way Comes* (1962), *R is for Rocket* (1962) and *Nemo* (1964).

INTRODUCTION - *Fahrenheit 451*

This unit has been designed to develop students' reading, writing, thinking, and language skills through exercises and activities related to *Fahrenheit 451* by Ray Bradbury. It includes eighteen lessons, supported by extra resource materials.

The **introductory lesson** introduces students to one main theme of the novel through a bulletin board activity. Following the introductory activity, students are given a transition to explain how the activity relates to the book they are about to read. Following the transition, students are given the materials they will be using during the unit. At the end of the lesson, students begin the pre-reading work for the first reading assignment.

The **reading assignments** are approximately thirty pages each; some are a little shorter while others are a little longer. Students have approximately 15 minutes of pre-reading work to do prior to each reading assignment. This pre-reading work involves reviewing the study questions for the assignment and doing some vocabulary work for 8 to 10 vocabulary words they will encounter in their reading.

The **study guide questions** are fact-based questions; students can find the answers to these questions right in the text. These questions come in two formats: short answer or multiple choice. The best use of these materials is probably to use the short answer version of the questions as study guides for students (since answers will be more complete), and to use the multiple choice version for occasional quizzes. It might be a good idea to make transparencies of your answer keys for the overhead projector.

The **vocabulary work** is intended to enrich students' vocabularies as well as to aid in the students' understanding of the book. Prior to each reading assignment, students will complete a two-part worksheet for approximately 8 to 10 vocabulary words in the upcoming reading assignment. Part I focuses on students' use of general knowledge and contextual clues by giving the sentence in which the word appears in the text. Students are then to write down what they think the words mean based on the words' usage. Part II nails down the definitions of the words by giving students dictionary definitions of the words and having students match the words to the correct definitions based on the words' contextual usage. Students should then have an understanding of the words when they meet them in the text.

After each reading assignment, students will go back and formulate answers for the study guide questions. Discussion of these questions serves as a **review** of the most important events and ideas presented in the reading assignments.

After the reading, a lesson is devoted to the **extra discussion questions/writing assignments**. These questions focus on interpretation, critical analysis and personal response, employing a variety of thinking skills and adding to the students' understanding of the novel.

Following the discussion, there is a **vocabulary review** lesson which pulls together all of the fragmented vocabulary lists for the reading assignments and gives students a review of all of the words they have studied.

The **group activity** which follows the discussion questions has students working in small groups to create a presentation about what they think the world will be like in 50 years.

There are three **writing assignments** in this unit, each with the purpose of informing, persuading, or having students express personal opinions. The first assignment is to inform: students create a fire escape plan for their homes. The second assignment is to express personal opinions: students tell what they think the future will be like (as a preparation for the group activity). The third assignment is to persuade: students persuade the teacher that today is better than 50 years from now will be or vice versa.

In addition, there is a **nonfiction reading assignment**. Students are required to read a piece of nonfiction related in some way to *Fahrenheit 451*. After reading their nonfiction pieces, students will fill out a worksheet on which they answer questions regarding facts, interpretation, criticism, and personal opinions.

The **review lesson** pulls together all of the aspects of the unit. The teacher is given four or five choices of activities or games to use which all serve the same basic function of reviewing all of the information presented in the unit.

The **unit test** comes in two formats: short answer or multiple choice. As a convenience, two different tests for each format have been included. There is also an advanced short answer unit test for higher level students.

There are additional **support materials** included with this unit. The **extra activities packet** includes suggestions for an in-class library, crossword and word search puzzles related to the novel, and extra vocabulary worksheets. There is a list of **bulletin board ideas** which gives the teacher suggestions for bulletin boards to go along with this unit. In addition, there is a list of **extra class activities** the teacher could choose from to enhance the unit or as a substitution for an exercise the teacher might feel is inappropriate for his/her class. **Answer keys** are located directly after the **reproducible student materials** throughout the unit. The student materials may be reproduced for use in the teacher's classroom without infringement of copyrights. No other portion of this unit may be reproduced without the written consent of Teacher's Pet Publications, Inc.

UNIT OBJECTIVES - *Fahrenheit 451*

1. Students will discuss the ideas of censorship and freedom of speech.

2. Students will demonstrate their understanding of the text on four levels: factual, interpretive, critical and personal.

3. Students will discuss the imagery used in the novel.

4. Students will create a world of the future.

5. Students will create a fire escape plan for their own homes.

6. Students will be given the opportunity to practice reading aloud and silently to improve their skills in each area.

7. Students will answer questions to demonstrate their knowledge and understanding of the main events and characters in *Fahrenheit 451* as they relate to the author's theme development.

8. Students will enrich their vocabularies and improve their understanding of the novel through the vocabulary lessons prepared for use in conjunction with the novel.

9. The writing assignments in this unit are geared to several purposes:
> a. To have students demonstrate their abilities to inform, to persuade, or to express their own personal ideas
> > Note: Students will demonstrate ability to write effectively to <u>inform </u>by developing and organizing facts to convey information. Students will demonstrate the ability to write effectively to <u>persuade</u> by selecting and organizing relevant information, establishing an argumentative purpose, and by designing an appropriate strategy for an identified audience. Students will demonstrate the ability to write effectively to <u>express personal ideas</u> by selecting a form and its appropriate elements.
>
> b. To check the students' reading comprehension
> c. To make students think about the ideas presented by the novel
> d. To encourage logical thinking
> e. To provide an opportunity to practice good grammar and improve students' use of the English language.

10. Students will read aloud, report, and participate in large and small group discussions to improve their public speaking and personal interaction skills.

READING ASSIGNMENT SHEET - *Fahrenheit 451*

Date Assigned	RA #	Assignment	Completion Date
	1	Beginning to "But it was late- and the arrival of his train put a stop to his plan."	
	2	From "The flutter of cards, motion of hands, of eyelids, the drone of the time-voice in the firehouse ceiling. . ." to the end of Part One	
	3	All of Part Two	
	4	All of Part Three	

RA # = Reading Assignment Number

UNIT OUTLINE - *Fahrenheit 451*

1	2	3	4	5
Introduction PV RA#1	Practice Reading	Read RA 1	Study ?s RA1 PVR RA2	Writing Assignment #1
6	**7**	**8**	**9**	**10**
Study ?s RA2 PVR RA3	Study ?s RA3 PVR RA4	Study ?s RA4 Extra ?s	Writing Assignment #2	Vocabulary
11	**12**	**13**	**14**	**15**
Group Activity	Group Activity	Nonfiction Reports	Censorship	Future Worlds
16	**17**	**18**		
Writing Assignment #3	Review	Test		

Key: P = Preview Study Questions   V = Prereading Vocabulary Worksheets R = Read RA = Reading Assignment

This page is left blank for two-sided printing.

STUDY GUIDE QUESTIONS

This page is left blank for two-sided printing.

SHORT ANSWER STUDY GUIDE QUESTIONS - *Fahrenheit 451*

Reading Assignment #1
1. Identify Guy Montag and describe his job.
2. Describe Clarisse McClellan.
3. What smelled like perfume to Montag?
4. Clarisse asked Montag if he was happy. Was he?
5. Who is Mildred, and what happened to her?
6. Why did Emergency Hospital send technicians instead of doctors to treat Mildred?
7. What are parlor-walls?
8. Describe the mechanical hound.
9. What did Montag believe had been done to the hound?
10. Why was Clarisse considered anti-social?
11. Who gave Clarisse most of her information about the way life used to be?

Reading Assignment #2
1. Who was Captain Beatty?
2. How did the firemen know which houses had books?
3. What lie did Captain Beatty tell Montag?
4. What did Montag do in the old lady's attic?
5. Why were the alarms to burn always at night?
6. Why did the old woman light the match and commit suicide?
7. What happened to Clarisse? Was it an accident?
8. What was Montag afraid Captain Beatty would discover when he came to visit?
9. Why did Captain Beatty believe books should be destroyed?
10. What did Montag show Mildred after the captain had left the house?

Reading Assignment 3
1. Who was Faber?
2. Why did Montag go to see Faber?
3. What three elements did Faber feel were missing from life?
4. What plan did Montag and Faber devise?
5. What was Montag willing to do to convince Faber to help carry out the plan?
6. What had Faber designed that allowed him to be in constant contact with Montag?
7. Why did Faber decide to go to St. Louis?
8. Why did Montag burn the book of poetry in the wall incinerator in his home?
9. Where did Montag hide his books after the ladies left?
10. What was the destination of the alarm on the night Montag returned to work at the firehouse?

Fahrenheit 451 Short Answer Study Questions Page 2

<u>Reading Assignment 4</u>
1. Who was the informant on Montag's home?
2. Why did Montag kill Captain Beatty?
3. Why didn't Montag run away before he killed Captain Beatty?
4. Where did Montag go after he killed Beatty?
5. When Montag left Faber's house, which direction did he go?
6. Why did Montag take whiskey, a suitcase, and some of Faber's dirty clothes with him?
7. What did the railroad tracks mean to Montag?
8. What was different about the fire Montag saw after leaving the river?
9. During the manhunt for Montag by the hound, why did the camera identify an innocent man as Montag?
10. What was different about the hobos Montag Met? Why did each man identify himself as a famous author or piece of literature?
11. What had Montag been able to memorize?
12. What happened to the city during the war?
13. What did Montag and the intellectuals believe their mission to be once the war ended?

ANSWER KEY: SHORT ANSWER STUDY GUIDE QUESTIONS - *Fahrenheit 451*

Reading Assignment #1

1. Identify Guy Montag and describe his job.
    Guy Montag is a fireman, a person who finds books and burns them.

2. Describe Clarisse McClellan.
    She is an unusual person, a young girl who liked to think and talk.

3. What smelled like perfume to Montag? The kerosine smelled like perfume to him.

4. Clarisse asked Montag if he was happy. Was he? No, he was not.

5. Who is Mildred, and what happened to her?
    Mildred is Montag's wife. She had taken an overdose of sleeping pills. Her stomach and blood had to be pumped clean.

6. Why did Emergency Hospital send technicians instead of doctors to treat Mildred?
    Suicide by this method was so common that technician-operated machines were developed to treat the patient.

7. What are parlor-walls?
    They are a kind of surround-television with which the audience can interact.

8. Describe the mechanical hound.
    It is a robot type of dog, equipped with a steel needle, and programmed to hunt and kill.

9. What did Montag believe had been done to the hound?
    He believed that the hound's memory had been programmed to act against him.

10. Why was Clarisse considered anti-social?
    She was part of the old society where talking and thinking were appreciated.

11. Who gave Clarisse most of her information about the way life used to be?
    Her uncle did.

<u>Reading Assignment #2</u>
1. Who was Captain Beatty?
   He was Montag's boss at the firehouse.

2. How did the firemen know which houses had books?
   Neighbors, friends and family members became informants and telephoned the information to the firemen.

3. What lie did Captain Beatty tell Montag?
   He told Montag that firemen had never been used to prevent fires, only to start them.

4. What did Montag do in the old lady's attic?
   He took a book.

5. Why were the alarms to burn always at night?
   The fires were prettier to watch and provided more of a show at night.

6. Why did the old woman light the match and commit suicide?
   She felt like life was not worth living without her books.

7. What happened to Clarisse? Was it an accident?
   She was hit by a car. The elimination of Clarisse was a part of the on-going operation of destroying the old society.

8. What was Montag afraid Captain Beatty would discover when he came to visit?
   He was afraid the captain would find the book he had taken from the old woman's attic.

9. Why did Captain Beatty believe books should be destroyed?
   He thought that they put upsetting thoughts in people's minds and kept them from being happy and satisfied.

10. What did Montag show Mildred after the captain had left the house?
    He showed her the books he had been stealing and hiding in the house.

<u>Reading Assignment 3</u>
1. Who was Faber?
   He was a retired English professor Montag had met in the park.

2. Why did Montag go to see Faber?
   He needed a duplicate copy of the stolen book before he returned the original to Captain Beatty.

3. What three elements did Faber feel were missing from life?
   He thought quality and texture of information, leisure time to think, and the right to carry out actions based on the other two items were missing.

4. What plan did Montag and Faber devise?
   They were going to plant books in firemen's homes and turn in alarms on the firemen. This was to cast suspicion on all firemen.

5. What was Montag willing to do to convince Faber to help carry out the plan?
   He would destroy his book, page by page until Faber would cooperate.

6. What had Faber designed that allowed him to be in constant contact with Montag?
   They had designed an electronic radio transmitter which could be placed in the ear.

7. Why did Faber decide to go to St. Louis?
   He wanted to enlist the help of an unemployed printer to begin making copies of books.

8. Why did Montag burn the book of poetry in the wall incinerator in his home?
   He had made a mistake by showing Mildred's friends that he had a book. Faber gave him orders through the radio transmitter to burn the book, to convince the ladies that he was playing a joke on them.

9. Where did Montag hide his books after the ladies left?
   He hid the books in his back yard.

10. What was the destination of the alarm on the night Montag returned to work at the firehouse?
    The alarm destination was Montag's home.

Reading Assignment 4
1. Who was the informant on Montag's home?
   Mildred's friends called in the first alarm, but Mildred called in the final alarm herself.

2. Why did Montag kill Captain Beatty?
   Captain Beatty was aware that Montag was wearing a radio transmitter, and he was determined to find out who was on the other end.

3. Why didn't Montag run away before he killed Captain Beatty?
   He knew that the mechanical hound was in the neighborhood and would kill him.

4. Where did Montag go after he killed Beatty?
   He went to Faber's house.

5. When Montag left Faber's house, which direction did he go?
   He headed for the river.

6. Why did Montag take whiskey, a suitcase, and some of Faber's dirty clothes with him?
    He needed some strong-smelling things to throw the dogs off of his own scent.

7. What did the railroad tracks mean to Montag?
    They were his path to follow to safety in the countryside.

8. What was different about the fire Montag saw after leaving the river?
    This fire was giving warmth and comfort, not destroying things.

9. During the manhunt for Montag by the hound, why did the camera identify an innocent man as Montag?
    The firemen needed a neat ending to the day's events. It was more important to have a dead body than to have the right person. It wouldn't do for the criminal to have outwitted the authorities and to have escaped; that would look bad.

10. What was different about the hobos Montag Met? Why did each man identify himself as a famous author or piece of literature?
    These men were all intellectuals and each had memorized a piece of literature to be written down at a later time.

11. What had Montag been able to memorize?
    He memorized the Book of Ecclesiastes.

12. What happened to the city during the war?
    The city and its inhabitants were destroyed.

13. What did Montag and the intellectuals believe their mission to be once the war ended?
    They wanted to learn from previous mistakes and always to remember.

Reading Assignment #1

1. Who is Guy Montag?
    a. He is a librarian.
    b. He is the mayor.
    c. He is a doctor.
    d. He is a fireman.

2. Describe Guy's job.
    a. He maintains information files for the city.
    b. He teaches school.
    c. He finds books and burns them.
    d. He is a curator in a museum.

3. Describe Clarisse McClellan.
    a. She is shy and slightly handicapped.
    b. She is a young girl who likes to think and talk.
    c. She is extremely rigid and law-abiding.
    d. She is a flirt whose only concern is getting men to like her.

4. What smelled like perfume to Montag?
    a. It was the printers ink on the books.
    b. It was the cooking fumes from the restaurant.
    c. It was the kerosene.
    d. It was the smoke from the fireplace.

5. Clarisse asked Montag a question. His reply was, "No." What was the question?
    a. Was he happy?
    b. Could he read?
    c. Did he ever want to get married?
    d. Had he ever committed a crime?

6. Who is Mildred?
    a. She is Clarisse's mother.
    b. She is Montag's wife.
    c. She is a doctor at Emergency Hospital.
    d. She is a writer who has gone underground.

7. What happened to Mildred?
    a. She was captured and sent to a prison camp.
    b. She contracted a fatal, contagious disease and had to be quarantined.
    c. She took an overdose of sleeping pills and had to have her stomach and blood pumped clean.
    d. She had just been promoted to a position of power in the government.

8. Why did Emergency Hospital send technicians instead of a doctor to treat the patient?
     a. The patient didn't have enough insurance coverage to merit a doctor's care.
     b. Doctors only treated men.
     c. There weren't enough doctors, so none ever left the hospital.
     d. That kind of medical procedure was so common that technician-operated machines had been developed to treat the patient.

9. What were parlor walls?
     a. They were a kind of surround television with which the audience could interact.
     b. They were portable partitions that could be repositioned to create a variety of living spaces.
     c. They were hidden microphones that could monitor conversations.
     d. They were barricades that separated one neighborhood from another.

10. There was a robotic animal equipped with a steel needle, and programmed to hunt and kill. What kind of animal was it?
     a. It was dragon.
     b. It was a hound.
     c. It was a lion.
     d. It was a rattlesnake.

11. What did Montag believe had been done to the animal?
     a. It had been programmed to beg for money.
     b. It had been programmed to do tricks.
     c. It had been programmed to attack the elderly.
     d. It had been programmed to act against Montag.

12. Clarisse was part of the old society where talking and thinking were appreciated. How was this viewed by the others?
     a. She was revered as a holy one.
     b. She was thought to be insane.
     c. She was considered anti-social.
     d. She was tolerated with amusement.

13. Where did Clarisse get most of her information about the way life used to be?
     a. Her uncle told her.
     b. She watched old videos.
     c. She learned it in history class.
     d. She had secretly read her grandmother's diaries, which she had hidden in her room.

Fahrenheit 451 Multiple Choice Study Guide Questions Page Three

Reading Assignment #2
14. Who was Captain Beatty?
    a. He was Montag's boss at work.
    b. He was a retired naval officer. He often told old sea stories.
    c. He was the mayor.
    d. He was Clarisse's uncle.

15. How did the firemen know which houses had books?
    a. The books all had bar codes on the back covers. These could be read for up to one mile away by a special computerized track.
    b. Neighbors, family members, and friends became informants and telephoned the authorities.
    c. They conducted random searches.
    d. The fire dogs could sniff them out.

16. What lie did Captain Beatty tell Montag?
    a. He told Montag that authors had never been appreciated; indeed, they had always been regarded as outcasts.
    b. He told Montag that women were too delicate to be workers.
    c. He told Montag that firemen had never been used to prevent fires, only to start them.
    d. He told Montag that he (Montag) was next in line for a promotion at work.

17. What did Montag do in the old lady's attic?
    a. He took a book.
    b. He sat and cried.
    c. He destroyed all of her old family pictures.
    d. He took a nap.

18. The firemen wanted to provide as much of a show as possible. How did they do this?
    a. They made watching mandatory for everyone over the age of twelve.
    b. They advertised by having volunteers call people to remind them to come.
    c. They had a famous person start the blaze.
    d. They had the fires at night when they look prettier.

19. What did the old woman do?
    a. She locked herself in her apartment and refused to watch.
    b. She lit the match and then committed suicide.
    c. She danced and threw more books on the blaze.
    d. She dressed in black, knelt before the fire, and prayed and cried.

20. What happened to Clarrise?
    a. She was hit by a car.
    b. She was hypnotized and forced to change her thinking.
    c. She was attacked by a pack of mechanical hounds.
    d. She escaped to the wilderness and joined the rebels.

21. What was Montag afraid would happen when the Captain came to visit?
    a. He was afraid the Captain would eat all of his (Montag's) food rations for the whole week.
    b. He was afraid the Captain would see how well he (Montag) was living, and reduce his pay.
    c. He was afraid the Captain would find the book he had stolen from the old lady.
    d. He was afraid the Captain would stay for a long visit. Montag was shy, and was very nervous about having guests.

22. What did Captain Beatty believe?
    a. He believed that all people should be masters of their own destinies.
    b. He believed that books put upsetting thoughts in people's minds and kept them from being happy and satisfied.
    c. He believed that firemen should be the highest paid workers because they were doing the most important job in society.
    d. He believed that the world was about to end because of all of the greed and corruption. He also believed that he could save it if enough people would follow him.

23. What did Montag do after the captain had left the house?
    a. He sat and cried.
    b. He disinfected everything the captain had touched.
    c. He went out for a long walk.
    d. He showed Mildred the books he had been stealing and hiding.

Reading Assignment 3

24. Who was Faber?
    a. He was Montag's brother-in-law, and another sympathizer.
    b. He was second in command after Beatty.
    c. He was a retired English professor.
    d. He was the chief physician at Emergency Hospital.

25. Why did Montag go to see Faber?
    a. He needed a duplicate copy of the stolen book before he returned the original to Captain Beatty.
    b. Faber had been a friend of Montag's wife's family. Montag thought Faber could give him advice about how to help his wife.
    c. He wanted Faber to translate the books that were not in English.
    d. He wanted to get information about others who had books. He thought that giving the information to Beatty might help his career.

26. Faber felt that three elements were missing from life. Which of these was NOT one of the elements?
    a. Quality and texture of information
    b. The satisfaction of choosing one's own job
    c. Leisure time to think
    d. The right to carry out actions based on the other two items

27. What plan did Montag and Faber devise?
    a. They were going to replace the kerosene with a non-flammable liquid.
    b. They were going to develop a virus to implant in the mechanical hounds. It would destroy their killer instincts.
    c. They were going to plant books in firemen's houses and turn in alarms on the firemen. This was to cast suspicion on all firemen.
    d. They were going to bury as many books as they could find in an old root cellar on Faber's property.

28. What was Montag willing to do to convince Faber to help carry out the plan?
    a. He would pay Faber the money his wife wanted to use for the fourth parlor wall.
    b. He would quit his job and move in with Faber.
    c. He would destroy his book, page by page, until Faber would cooperate.
    d. He would do the first five operations by himself so that Faber would not be implicated.

29. What had Faber designed that allowed him to be in constant contact with Montag? a. He had designed a TV monitor that could be placed in a watch mechanism.
    b. He had designed an electronic radio transmitter which could be placed in the ear.
    c. He had installed a thought-wave amplifier in each of their brains.
    d. He had invented a liquid that could be traced by monitoring it's position emissions.

30. Why did Faber decide to go to St. Louis?
    a. He wanted to get away from Montag for a while.
    b. He wanted to raise funds for their project.
    c. He needed electronic parts and St. Louis was the only place to buy them.
    d. He wanted to enlist the help of an unemployed printer to begin making copies of books.

31. Why did Montag burn the book of poetry in the wall incinerator in his home?
    a. He had been told to do so by Faber, through the transmitter, to show the ladies he was playing a joke on them.
    b. He was desperate enough to do anything to save his relationship with his wife.
    c. He didn't like the poems. He though they weren't worth saving.
    d. He was addicted to the feelings of pain/pleasure that he got from burning books.

32. Where did Montag hide his books after the ladies left?
    a. He hid them in his attic, above the heat/air conditioning vent.
    b. He hid them behind a false wall he had previously built in his apartment for such a time.
    c. He hid them in his backyard.
    d. He hid them in the firehouse.

33. What was the destination of the alarm on the night Montag returned to work at the firehouse?
    a. The destination was the town library.
    b. The destination was Montag's home.
    c. The destination was the hospital. A few of the doctors were giving books to the patients.
    d. It was Faber's home.

Reading Assignment 4

34. Who was the final informant on Montag's home?
    a. It was Faber.
    b. It was Mildred.
    c. It was Beatty.
    d. It was Mrs. Phelps.

35. Why did Montag kill Captain Beatty?
    a. Montag was insane because he saw his books burning.
    b. It was an accident, Montag's finger slipped on the safety catch on the flame thrower, and Beatty got in the way.
    c. Beatty was aware that Montag was wearing a radio transmitter, and he was determined to find out who was on the other end.
    d. He wanted to stop the firemen from burning more books.

36. Why didn't Montag run away before he killed Captain Beatty?
    a. He wanted to stay and watch his house and books burn totally into ashes.
    b. Faber told him to stay where he was.
    c. He wanted to make sure Mildred was safe.
    d. He knew that the mechanical hound was in the neighborhood and would kill him.

37. Where did Montag go after he killed Beatty?
    a. He went to the firehouse.
    b. He went to Faber's house.
    c. He went to Mildred's friend's house.
    d. He went for a long, fast ride in his beetle.

38. When Montag left Faber's house, which direction did he go?
    a. He headed back into the city.
    b. He headed across the state to the mountains.
    c. He headed for the river.
    d. He headed for the spaceport.

39. Why did Montag take whiskey, a suitcase, and some of Faber's dirty clothes with him?
    a. He needed some strong-smelling things to throw the dogs off his scent.
    b. He wanted to disguise himself as a drunken bum so he could pass through the city.
    c. He wanted to leave them at a deserted shack to make his pursuers think he was in one location while he went the opposite direction.
    d. He was headed into the wilderness. He took the whiskey in case he needed it for pain; the dirty clothes to wear, and the suitcase to collect any books he might find along the way.

40. Montag identified something he saw in his travels as a path to safety. What was it?
    a. It was the North Star.
    b. It was the lights from the airport runway.
    c. It was the railroad tracks.
    d. It was a series of road signs.

41. What was different about the fire Montag saw after leaving the river?
    a. It was a different color because it was fueled by natural wood instead of chemicals.
    b. It was giving warmth and comfort, not destroying things.
    c. It was considerably cooler than the fires that the firemen ignited.
    d. It was only giving off low flames. Those started by the firemen usually leaped hundreds of feet into the air.

42. During the manhunt for Montag by the hound, why did the camera identify an innocent man as Montag?
    a. Faber deliberately misled them to get them off of Montag's trail.
    b. The computer that was tracking him malfunctioned and identified the wrong man.
    c. Nobody really knew what he looked like, so they didn't know whom to chase.
    d. The firemen needed to look good, and put a neat ending on the day's work.

43. What was different about the hobos Montag Met?
    a. They were all disfigured from exposure to the unfiltered country air.
    b. They were all former firemen.
    c. They were all intellectuals.
    d. They were clean and well-fed.

44. How were these men preserving literature?
    a. They had built a secret fireproof library underground and quietly collected books.
    b. Each carried a backpack full of books. It was his duty to safeguard them.
    c. They were burying books in holes along the railroad tracks. They had developed a secret marking system so they knew where the books were.
    d. Each man had memorized a piece of literature to be written down at a later time.

45. What literature did Montag preserve?
    a. It was War and Peace.
    b. It was the Book of Ecclesiastes.
    c. It was the Constitution of the United States.
    d. It was all of Shakespeare's plays.

46. What happened during the war?
    a. The city was damaged, but not seriously.
    b. They were victorious and destroyed the other cities.
    c. The city and its inhabitants were destroyed.
    d. Both sides called a truce, and together pursued the destruction of all books.

47. What did Montag and the intellectuals believe their mission to be once the war was ended?
    a. They wanted to learn from previous mistakes and always to remember.
    b. They wanted to convert any survivors to their way of thinking.
    c. They wanted to teach everyone how to read.
    d. They wanted to pursue and kill any remaining firemen so they couldn't start burning books again.

ANSWER KEY - MULTIPLE CHOICE STUDY/QUIZ QUESTIONS
Fahrenheit 451

Reading Assignment No. 1

1. D
2. C
3. B
4. C
5. A
6. B
7. C
8. D
9. A
10. B
11. D
12. C

Reading Assignment No. 2

13. A
14. A
15. B
16. C
17. A
18. D
19. B
20. A
21. C
22. B
23. D

Reading Assignment No. 3

24. C
25. A
26. B
27. C
28. C
29. B
30. D
31. A
32. C
33. B

Reading Assignment No. 4

34. B
35. C
36. D
37. B
38. C
39. A
40. C
41. B
42. D
43. C
44. D
45. B
46. C
47. A

PREREADING VOCABULARY WORKSHEETS

This page is left blank for two-sided printing.

VOCABULARY WORKSHEETS - *Fahrenheit 451*

Part I: Using Prior Knowledge and Contextual Clues - Reading Assignment
 Below are the sentences in which the vocabulary words appear in the text. Read the sentence. Use any clues you can find in the sentence combined with your prior knowledge, and write what you think the underlined words mean in the spaces provided.

1. With his symbolic helmet number 451 on his stolid head...he flicked the igniter and the house jumped up in a gorging fire.

2. Impossible: for how many people did you know that refracted your own light to you.

3. And if the muscles of his jaws stretched imperceptibly, she would yawn long before he would.

4. He felt that the stars had been pulverized by the sound of the black jets and that in the morning the earth would be covered with their dust like a strange snow.

5. And the men with the cigarettes in their straight-lined mouths, the men with the eyes of puff adders, took up their load of machine and tube, their case of liquid melancholy and the slow dark sludge of nameless stuff, and strolled out the door.

6. Light flickered on bits of ruby glass and on sensitive capillary hairs in the Nylon-brushed nostrils of the creature...

7. Below, the Hound had sunk back down upon its eight incredible insect legs and was humming to itself again, it multifaceted eyes at peace.

8. It's like a lesson in ballistics. It has a trajectory we decide on for it.

Fahrenheit 451 Vocabulary for Reading Assignment 1 Continued

Part II: Determining the Meaning
        Match the vocabulary words to their dictionary definitions. If there are words for which you cannot figure out the definition by contextual clues and by process of elimination, look them up in a dictionary.

___ 1. stolid
___ 2. refracted
___ 3. imperceptibly
___ 4. pulverized
___ 5. melancholy
___ 6. capillary
___ 7. multifaceted
___ 8. ballistics

A. Sadness; gloominess
B. The study of the dynamics of projectiles
C. Having or revealing little emotion
D. Having many faces
E. Deflected from a straight path
F. Impossible to detect by ordinary senses
G. Fine; small in diameter
H. Reduced to powder

Fahrenheit 451 Vocabulary for Reading Assignment No. 2

Part I: Using Prior Knowledge and Contextual Clues
        Below are the sentences in which the vocabulary words appear in the text. Read the sentence. Use any clues you can find in the sentence combined with your prior knowledge, and write what you think the underlined words mean in the spaces provided.

1. . . . all the sounds came to Montag, behind the barrier he had momentarily <u>erected</u>.

2. Were all firemen picked then for their looks as well as their <u>proclivities</u>?

3. Beatty, Stoneman, and Black ran up the sidewalk, suddenly <u>odious</u> and fat in their plump fireproof slickers.

4. He felt one hand and then the other work his coat free and let it slump to the floor. . . . His hands were <u>ravenous</u>. And his eyes were beginning to feel hunger, as if they must look at something, anything, everything.

5. "Life becomes one big <u>pratfall</u>, Montag; everything bang, boff, and wow!"

6. There was no <u>dictum</u>, no declaration, no censorship, to start with, no!

7. Cram them full of <u>noncombustible</u> data, chock them so damned full of 'facts' they feel stuffed, but absolutely 'brilliant' with information.

8. I'll think I'm responding to the play, when it's only a <u>tactile</u> reaction to vibration.

Fahrenheit 451 Vocabulary for Reading Assignment No. 2 Continued

Part II: Determining the Meaning
     Now match the vocabulary words to their dictionary definitions. If there are words for which you cannot figure out the definition by contextual clues and by process of elimination, look them up in a dictionary.

___ 1. erected	A. Authoritative pronouncement
___ 2. proclivities	B. Relating to the sense of touch
___ 3. odious	C. Set up; established
___ 4. ravenous	D. Humiliating failure; a fall on the buttocks
___ 5. pratfall	E. Predispositions; tendencies
___ 6. dictum	F. Does not burn easily
___ 7. noncombustible	G. Arousing strong dislike or displeasure
___ 8. tactile	H. Extremely hungry; greedy for gratification

Fahrenheit 451 Vocabulary for Reading Assignment No. 3

Part I: Using Prior Knowledge and Contextual Clues
      Below are the sentences in which the vocabulary words appear in the text. Read the sentence. Use any clues you can find in the sentence combined with your prior knowledge, and write what you think the underlined words mean in the spaces provided.

1. . . . he talked in a <u>cadenced</u> voice. . . and when an hour had passed he said something to Montag and Montag sensed it was a rhymeless poem.

2. The train radio vomited upon Montag, in <u>retaliation</u>, a great tonload of music made of tin, copper, silver, chromium and brass.

3. Books were only one type of <u>receptacle</u> where we stored a lot of things we were afraid we might forget.

4. Proof of my terrible <u>cowardice</u>.

5. On one wall a woman smiled and drank orange juice <u>simultaneously</u>. How does she do both at once, thought Montag . . .

6. For these were the hands that had acted on their own, no part of him, here was where the conscience first <u>manifested</u> itself to snatch books, dart off with Job and Ruth and Willie Shakespeare, and now, in the firehouse, these hands seemed gloved with blood.

7. You towered with rage, yelled quotes at me, I calmly <u>parried </u>every thrust. *Power*, I said.

Fahrenheit 451 Vocabulary for Reading Assignment No. 3 Continued

8. The folly of mistaking a metaphor for a proof, a torrent of <u>verbiage</u> for a spring of capital truths, and oneself as a oracle, is inborn in us, Mr. Valery once said.

Part II: Determining the Meaning

     You have tried to figure out the meanings of the vocabulary words for Reading Assignment No. 3. Now match the vocabulary words to their dictionary definitions. If there are words for which you cannot figure out the definition by contextual clues and by process of elimination, look them up in a dictionary.

___ 1. cadenced	A. Returning like for like
___ 2. retaliation	B. Wordiness
___ 3. receptacle	C. Showed; revealed
___ 4. cowardice	D. Deflected; avoided
___ 5. simultaneously	E. With a rhythmic flow
___ 6. manifested	F. Ignoble fear in the face of danger
___ 7. verbiage	G. A container that holds matter
___ 8. parried	H. At the same time

Fahrenheit 451 Vocabulary for Reading Assignment No. 4

Part I: Using Prior Knowledge and Contextual Clues
    Below are the sentences in which the vocabulary words appear in the text. Read the sentence. Use any clues you can find in the sentence combined with your prior knowledge, and write what you think the underlined words mean in the spaces provided.

1. The other firemen waited behind him, in the darkness, their faces illumined faintly by the smouldering foundation.

2. The other was like a chunk of burnt pinelog he was carrying along as penance for some obscure sin.

3. Two dozen of them flurried, wavering, indecisive, three miles off.

4. And there on the small screen was the burnt house, and the crowd and something with a sheet over it and out of the sky, fluttering, came the helicopter like a grotesque flower.

5. . . . Montag might . . . see himself dramatized, described, made over, standing there, limned in the bright small television screen from outside . . . .

6. He saw a great juggernaut of stars form in the sky and threaten to roll over and crush him.

7. He smelled the heavy musk like perfume mingled with blood and the gummed exhalation of the animal's breath, all cardamon and moss and ragweed odor in this huge night where the trees ran at him . . . .

Fahrenheit 451 Vocabulary for Reading Assignment No. 4 Continued

8. The most important single thing we had to pound into ourselves is that we were not important; we mustn't be <u>pedants</u>; we were not to feel superior to anyone else in the world.

9. There was a silly damn bird called a Phoenix back before Christ; every few hundred years he built a <u>pyre</u> and burned himself up.

Part II: Determining the Meaning

___ 1. smouldering
___ 2. obscure
___ 3. indecisive
___ 4. grotesque
___ 5. limned
___ 6. juggernaut
___ 7. cardamon
___ 8. pedants
___ 9. pyre

A. Indian spice
B. Those who flaunt their knowledge
C. Described
D. Not able to make a decision
E. A pile of combustible materials for burning a corpse
F. Bizarre; distorted
G. Burning with little smoke and no flame
H. Overwhelmingly advancing sight crushing all in its path
I. Not clear; partially hidden; remote

Reading Assignment No. 1
1.　C
2.　E
3.　F
4.　H
5.　A
6.　G
7.　D
8.　B

Reading Assignment No. 2
1.　C
2.　E
3.　G
4.　H
5.　D
6.　A
7.　F
8.　B

Reading Assignment No. 3
1.　E
2.　A
3.　G
4.　F
5.　H
6.　C
7.　B
8.　D

Reading Assignment No. 4
1.　G
2.　I
3.　D
4.　F
5.　C
6.　H
7.　A
8.　B
9.　E

This page is left blank for two-sided printing.

DAILY LESSONS

This page is left blank for two-sided printing.

LESSON ONE

Objectives
1. To introduce the *Fahrenheit 451* unit.
2. To distribute books and other related materials
3. To preview the study questions for Reading Assignment 1
4. To familiarize students with the vocabulary for Reading Assignment 1

Note: There are several introductory activities which could be done for this unit, depending on which ideas from the novel you wish to emphasize. Be sure to look in the Unit Resource Materials section of this unit for additional ideas regarding introductory activities.

For this particular introductory activity, have students each bring in a picture of something which represents a way to "escape" and post their pictures on the board as you do the discussion for Activity #1. This is a good way to get your bulletin board done if you are short on time, and it also gives students a physical way to contribute to your classroom. Something they have contributed will be on display.

Activity #1

Start by talking about the stresses people have in our society. Perhaps ask students what stresses they have in their own lives. Ask students to get out the pictures they have brought showing ways people escape, ways people deal with the pressures of life. Have each student explain the relevance of his picture, and post it on the bulletin board. After all the examples have been given, take a few minutes to discuss ways advertisers take advantage of our need to relax, our need to "escape." Follow up by asking what happens when people go too far in their escapes--when their minds and/or bodies go "on holiday" too long. Use this as a transition to introduce *Fahrenheit 451*.

Activity #2

Distribute the materials students will use in this unit. Explain in detail how students are to use these materials.

Study Guides Students should read the study guide questions for each reading assignment prior to beginning the reading assignment to get a feeling for what events and ideas are important in the section they are about to read. After reading the section, students will (as a class or individually) answer the questions to review the important events and ideas from that section of the book. Students should keep the study guides as study materials for the unit test.

Vocabulary Prior to reading a reading assignment, students will do vocabulary work related to the section of the book they are about to read. Following the completion of the reading of the book, there will be a vocabulary review of all the words used in the vocabulary assignments. Students should keep their vocabulary work as study materials for the unit test.

Reading Assignment Sheet   You need to fill in the reading assignment sheet to let students know by when their reading has to be completed. You can either write the assignment sheet up on a side blackboard or bulletin board and leave it there for students to see each day, or you can "ditto" copies for each student to have. In either case, you should advise students to become very familiar with the reading assignments so they know what is expected of them.

Extra Activities Center   The Extra Activities pages of this unit contain suggestions for an extra library of related books and articles in your classroom as well as crossword and word search puzzles. Make an extra activities center in your room where you will keep these materials for students to use. (Bring the books and articles in from the library and keep several copies of the puzzles on hand.) Explain to students that these materials are available for students to use when they finish reading assignments or other class work early.

Nonfiction Assignment Sheet   Explain to students that they each are to read at least one non-fiction piece related to the ideas presented in *Fahrenheit 451* at some time during the unit. Students will fill out a nonfiction assignment sheet after completing the reading to help you evaluate their reading experiences and to help the students think about and evaluate their own reading experiences.

Books   Each school has its own rules and regulations regarding student use of school books. Advise students of the procedures that are normal for your school.

Activity #3

Preview the study questions and have students do the vocabulary work for Reading Assignment 1 of *Fahrenheit 451*. If students do not finish this assignment during this class period, they should complete it prior to the next class meeting.

NONFICTION ASSIGNMENT SHEET
(To be completed after reading the required nonfiction article)

Name _____ Date _____

Title of Nonfiction Read _____

Written By _____ Publication Date _____

I. Factual Summary: Write a short summary of the piece you read.

II. Vocabulary
    1. With which vocabulary words in the piece did you encounter some degree of difficulty?

    2. How did you resolve your lack of understanding with these words?

III. Interpretation: What was the main point the author wanted you to get from reading his work?

IV. Criticism
    1. With which points of the piece did you agree or find easy to accept? Why?

    2. With which points of the piece did you disagree or find difficult to believe? Why?

V. Personal Response: What do you think about this piece? OR How does this piece influence your ideas?

LESSON TWO

<u>Objectives</u>
     1. To exercise students' memories
     2. To have an interesting way to begin reading this novel
     3. To show students how difficult it would actually be to memorize an entire book, as Montag and others will do in the novel

<u>Activity</u>
     Assign each student in your class a passage to memorize from the first reading assignment. Give students the remainder of the period to memorize their lines. If students seem to finish early, they may begin reciting their lines in order, to "put together" and "read" the first part of the novel.

PASSAGE ASSIGNMENTS - *Fahrenheit 451*

#	From:	To:
1	It was a pleasure to burn.	... wind turned dark with burning
2	Montag grinned the fierce grin ...	... as long as he remembered
3	He hung up his black beetle-colored helmet	... as if someone had called his name
4	The last few nights	... before he could focus his eyes or speak
5	But now tonight	... in the middle of the pavement waiting
6	The trees overhead made a great sound	"No, you don't," she said, in awe.
7	He felt she was walking in a circle	... so late in the year
8	There was only the girl walking with him now	... you're just a man, after all ...
9	He saw himself in her eyes	... the power might not come on again too soon
10	And then Clarisse McClellan said:	... He laughed.
11	She glanced quickly over.	You're changing the subject.
12	I sometimes think drivers don't know	... stretch the advertising out so it would last
13	I didn't know that!	... all its lights were blazing
14	What's going on?	Her front door shut gently.
15	Happy! Of all the nonsense.	... and <u>they</u> had talked. . . .
16	Montag shook his head.	... independent of will, habit, and conscience
17	He glanced back at the wall.	... own innermost trembling thought
18	What incredible power of identification	... so dammed late at night. . .
19	He opened the bedroom door	... so he could follow the tune
20	He felt his smile slide away	... and ask for it back
21	Without turning on the light	... gone down in it for the third time
22	The room was cold	... slid off in darkness
23	He stood very straight	Mildred!
24	Her face was like a snow-covered island	... in the light of the tiny flare
25	As he stood there the sky over the house	... plunge toward the telephone
26	The jets were gone.	... go on moving and moving
27	They had this machine	... other machine was working, too
28	The other machine, operated by an equally	... just gives up, just quits
29	Stop it!	... M.D. from Emergency
30	"Hell!" The operator's cigarette moved on his lip	So long.
31	And the men with the cigarettes	I never saw them before in my <u>life</u>
32	Half an hour passed.	If only . . .
33	He got up and put back the drapes	... their hypnotic web
34	Montag moved out through the French windows	... moving along at an easy pace
35	Well, after all, this is the age	... to form a silver cataract there
36	One drop of rain.	... dissolve on his tongue
37	At nine in the morning	... another piece of bread
38	Montag sat down	Don't you remember?
39	What? Did we have a wild party or something?	"You don't look so hot yourself," said his wife.

LESSON THREE

<u>Objectives</u>
>   1. To begin reading the novel
>   2. To evaluate students' memorization work

<u>Activity #1</u>
>   Have students speak the passages they have memorized, beginning with passage assignment 1 and working through the rest of the assignments. Evaluate students' presentations. (Give two grades; one for memorization and one for presentation.)

<u>Activity #2</u>
>   After the presentations are completed, have students read the remainder of Reading Assignment #1 silently in class. Be sure to tell them to complete this assignment prior to the next class period.

LESSON FOUR

Objectives
1. To review the main events and ideas from Reading Assignment 1
2. To preview the study questions for Reading Assignment 2
3. To familiarize students with the vocabulary in Reading Assignment 2
4. To read Reading Assignment 2

Activity #1

Give students a few minutes to formulate answers for the study guide questions for Reading Assignment 1, and then discuss the answers to the questions in detail. Write the answers on the board or overhead transparency so students can have the correct answers for study purposes. Note: It is a good practice in public speaking and leadership skills for individual students to take charge of leading the discussions of the study questions. Perhaps a different student could go to the front of the class and lead the discussion each day that the study questions are discussed during this unit. Of course, the teacher should guide the discussion when appropriate and be sure to fill in any gaps the students leave.

Activity #2

Give students about fifteen minutes to preview the study questions for Reading Assignment 2 of *Fahrenheit 451* and to do the related vocabulary work.

Activity #3

Assign students to read chapters 4-7 of *Fahrenheit 451* prior to your next class period. If there is time remaining in this period, students may begin reading silently.

LESSON FIVE

Objectives
1. To give students the opportunity to practice writing to inform
2. To help keep students and their families keep safe in case of fire in their homes
3. To promote logical thinking
4. To give the teacher the opportunity to evaluate students' writing skills

Activity #1

Distribute Writing Assignment #1. Discuss the directions in detail and give students ample time to complete the assignment.

Activity #2

If students finish the writing assignment early, they should either work on reading Reading Assignment #2 or their nonfiction reading assignments.

LESSON SIX

Objectives

      1. To check to see that students read Reading Assignment 2 as assigned

      2. To review the main ideas and events from Reading Assignment 2

      3. To preview the study questions for Reading Assignment 3

      4. To familiarize students with the vocabulary in Reading Assignment 3

      5. To read Reading Assignment 3

      6. To evaluate students' oral reading

Activity #1

      Quiz - Distribute quizzes and give students about 10 minutes to complete them. (Note: The quizzes may either be the short answer study guides or the multiple choice version for Reading Assignment 2.) Have students exchange papers. Grade the quizzes as a class. Collect the papers for recording the grades. (If you used the multiple choice version as a quiz, take a few minutes to discuss the answers for the short answer version if your students are using the short answer version for their study guides.)

Activity #2

      Give students about 15 minutes to preview the study questions for Reading Assignment 3 and do the related vocabulary work.

Activity #3

      Have students read Reading Assignment 3 orally for the remainder of the class period. If you have not given students a grade for oral reading this marking term, this would be a good opportunity to do so. An evaluation form in included with this unit for your convenience. If students do not complete reading this assignment during this class period, they should do so prior to your next class meeting.

WRITING ASSIGNMENT 1 - *Fahrenheit 451*

PROMPT

Fire has long been a fascinating thing for mankind. It can be useful; it can be pretty; it can keep us warm, but it can also be very dangerous. Every kid knows Smokey the Bear and has been advised how dangerous fire is to our wildlife friends. Everyone knows and fears the possibility of having a house fire while we are snuggled up in our beds at night. We are fortunate that modern technology has brought us sprinkling systems and fire alarms for our homes. The question then becomes, "What do we do when the smoke alarm goes off?"

Your assignment is to make and write down a fire escape plan for your family and your house. You must give written directions as well as make a map for occupants of each bedroom in your home.

PREWRITING

First of all, draw a little diagram of your house or apartment. It doesn't have to be perfect for this prewriting exercise. Locate the main rooms of your home. Think for a minute. Where would a fire be most likely to start? Probably in the kitchen, near a heating source, or near an area with a lot of electrical wiring. Locate these and any other areas in your home that are areas where a fire might be likely to start. Put an X on each of those areas.

Where are the bedrooms in your home in relation to the X marks? Find the best route of escape for the occupants of each of the bedrooms. Mark them on your diagram. If the X marks eliminate all routes of escape, deal with the X marks that are most likely to be trouble spots.

Think for a minute and make a list of the things that will need to be done to get everyone out safely. Next to each job, write down the name of the person who should be responsible for that job.

DRAFTING

Write an introductory paragraph telling the circumstances of the prospective fire. Write one paragraph for each member of your family, giving them simple, specific instructions as to what to do if there is a fire in your home while you are all in bed asleep. Each person should start from his or her own bedroom.

Write a concluding paragraph in which you give miscellaneous details about what rooms in your home should have fire extinguishers, rope ladders, or other emergency equipment.

Make a diagram of your house for each bedroom, and mark each bedroom's escape route on the diagram in a bright color so it can be easily seen.

PROOFREADING

When you finish the rough draft of your paper, ask a student who sits near you to read it. After reading your rough draft, he/she should tell you what he/she liked best about your work, which parts were difficult to understand, and ways in which your work could be improved. Reread your paper considering your critic's comments, and make the corrections you think are necessary.

ORAL READING EVALUATION - *Fahrenheit 451*

Name _____ Class____ Date _____

SKILL	EXCELLENT	GOOD	AVERAGE	FAIR	POOR
Fluency	5	4	3	2	1
Clarity	5	4	3	2	1
Audibility	5	4	3	2	1
Pronunciation	5	4	3	2	1
_____	5	4	3	2	1
_____	5	4	3	2	1

Total _____ Grade _____

Comments:

LESSON SEVEN

Objectives
1. To review the main events and ideas from Reading Assignment 3
2. To preview the study questions and vocabulary for Reading Assignment 4
3. To read Reading Assignment 4

Activity #1

Discuss the answers to the study guide questions for Reading Assignment 2. Jot down the answers to the questions on the board for students to copy for study use later.

Activity #2

Give students about 15 minutes to preview the study questions for Reading Assignment 4 and do the related vocabulary work.

Activity #3

Have students read Reading Assignment 4 for the remainder of the class period. If you have not completed the oral reading evaluations, use this class time to do so. If you have completed the evaluations, students may read silently. If students do not complete reading this assignment during this class period, they should do so prior to your next class meeting.

LESSON EIGHT

Objectives
1. To review the main ideas and events from chapters 26-31
2. To discuss *Fahrenheit 451* on interpretive and critical levels

Activity #1

Take a few minutes at the beginning of the period to review the study questions for Reading Assignment 4.

Activity #2

Choose the questions from the Extra Discussion Questions/Writing Assignments which seem most appropriate for your students. A class discussion of these questions is most effective if students have been given the opportunity to formulate answers to the questions prior to the discussion. To this end, you may either have all the students formulate answers to all the questions, divide your class into groups and assign one or more questions to each group, or you could assign one question to each student in your class. The option you choose will make a difference in the amount of class time needed for this activity.

Activity #3

After students have had ample time to formulate answers to the questions, begin your class discussion of the questions and the ideas presented by the questions. Be sure students take notes during the discussion so they have information to study for the unit test.

Interpretation

1. From what point of view is *Fahrenheit 451* written? Is this the best choice of ways to write this story? Explain why or why not.

2. If you were to rewrite *Fahrenheit 451* as a play, where would you start and end each act? Explain why.

3. What are the main conflicts in the novel? Are they resolved by the end of the book? If so, how? If not, why not?

4. Bradbury has repeatedly used words relating to fire. Find as many examples as you can in the book, and explain the effect of his word choices on us, the readers.

5. Why do you think Mr. Bradbury set his story in the city? In the story, what kinds of things happen in the city as opposed to the country?

6. Describe Captain Beatty's theory of how firemen began and why they were needed.

Critical

7. Describe Montag's relationship with Mildred.

8. Are Montag's actions believably motivated? Explain why or why not.

9. *Fahrenheit* is a relatively short novel. Could anything have been gained by including more scenes from the time before or after the events of this story? If so, what could have been added and for what purpose? If not, explain why not.

10. Characterize Ray Bradbury's style of writing. How does it contribute to the value of the novel?

11. Compare and contrast Mildred and Clarisse.

12. Compare and contrast Montag and Beatty.

13. Are the characters in *Fahrenheit 451* stereotypes? If so, explain why Ray Bradbury used stereotypes. If not, explain how the characters merit individuality.

14. Explain how the title relates to the events of the novel and the themes of *Fahrenheit 451*.

15. Explain Faber's role in the novel. Why was he included?

15. What was Clarisse's role in the novel? Why was she important?

Critical/Personal Response

17. Could the same thing happen to us today? Explain why or why not.

18. What do you think Faber meant when he said, "I don't talk things, sir. I talk the meaning of things. I sit here and know I am alive."

19. How would the story and its effect have changed if Montag had been caught and punished in the end.

20. Was Montag a hero?

21. Why was Montag's society so violent?

22. Why did there seem to be a low value placed on human life in the story?

23. What kinds of things do we have today that resemble things in Montag's society?

Personal Response

25. Did you enjoy reading *Fahrenheit 451*? Why or why not?

26. Are there informers in our society? If so, who are they? If not, why don't we have them?

27. Why do you think books were banned in Montag's society?

28. What does it mean to "live"? What kinds of things contribute to the quality of our lives?

29. Are there books that should be banned? If so, which ones, and why? If not, why not?

30. Would you be an informer if you lived in Montag's society?

LESSON NINE

Objectives

     1. To begin to prepare students for the group activity project which will be started in Lesson Eleven

     2. To give students the opportunity to be creative and to express their own opinions

     3. To give the teacher the opportunity to evaluate students' writing skills

     4. To get students to think about their futures, the future of our world

Activity #1

     Distribute Writing Assignment #2. Discuss the directions in detail and give students ample time to complete the assignment.

Activity #2

     While students are working on this writing assignment, call individual students to your desk for a writing conference about their first writing assignments. A writing evaluation form is included with this unit to help you structure your conferences, if you wish to use it.

LESSON TEN

Objective

     To review all of the vocabulary work done in this unit

Activity

     Choose one (or more) of the vocabulary review activities listed below and spend your class period as directed in the activity. Some of the materials for these review activities are located in the Vocabulary Resource section of this unit.

WRITING ASSIGNMENT #2 - *Fahrenheit 451*

PROMPT

In Ray Bradbury's *Fahrenheit 451* we have read about one possible scenario for the future. No one really knows how things will be in the future, but at one time or another we all think about it. What is your vision of the future? What do you think our world will be like 50 years from now?

Your assignment is to describe our world as you believe it will be 50 years from now.

PREWRITING

Choose five major topics for your composition--five areas of our lives you will describe. In other words, some areas to consider might be government, ecology, business, lifestyle, transportation, jobs/workplaces, economy, food, shelter, clothing, music, architecture, agriculture, entertainment, etc. Choose five of these or think up some of your own.

Make five columns on a piece of scratch paper and title each with one of your five topics. Under each topic, in the appropriate columns, jot down notes about how you think each will be in 50 years.

DRAFTING

Write a paragraph in which you introduce the idea that you believe life will be different in 50 years, especially in the areas you have chosen to write about (your five topics).

In the body of your composition, write one paragraph for each of your topics. Use a topic sentence to state exactly how you believe that topic will be different in 50 years, and then fill in your paragraph with specific examples you have notes about in your prewriting scratch paper column. Do that for each of your five topics.

Write a paragraph in which you summarize your ideas and conclude your composition.

PROMPT

When you finish the rough draft of your paper, ask a student who sits near you to read it. After reading your rough draft, he/she should tell you what he/she liked best about your work, which parts were difficult to understand, and ways in which your work could be improved. Reread your paper considering your critic's comments, and make the corrections you think are necessary.

PROOFREADING

Do a final proofreading of your paper double-checking your grammar, spelling, organization, and the clarity of your ideas.

WRITING EVALUATION FORM - *Fahrenheit 451*

Name _____ Date _____

Grade _____

Circle One For Each Item:

Grammar:	correct	errors noted on paper
Spelling:	correct	errors noted on paper
Punctuation:	correct	errors noted on paper
Legibility:	excellent	good fair poor

Strengths:

Weaknesses:

Comments/Suggestions:

VOCABULARY REVIEW ACTIVITIES - *Fahrenheit 451*

1. Divide your class into two teams and have an old-fashioned spelling or definition bee.

2. Give each of your students (or students in groups of two, three or four) a *Fahrenheit 451* Vocabulary Word Search Puzzle. The person (group) to find all of the vocabulary words in the puzzle first wins.

3. Give students a *Fahrenheit 451* Vocabulary Word Search Puzzle without the word list. The person or group to find the most vocabulary words in the puzzle wins.

4. Use a *Fahrenheit 451* Vocabulary Crossword Puzzle. Put the puzzle onto a transparency on the overhead projector (so everyone can see it), and do the puzzle together as a class.

5. Give students a *Fahrenheit 451* Vocabulary Matching Worksheet to do.

6. Divide your class into two teams. Use the *Fahrenheit 451* vocabulary words with their letters jumbled as a word list. Student 1 from Team A faces off against Student 1 from Team B. You write the first jumbled word on the board. The first student (1A or 1B) to unscramble the word wins the chance for his/her team to score points. If 1A wins the jumble, go to student 2A and give him/her a definition. He/she must give you the correct spelling of the vocabulary word which fits that definition. If he/she does, Team A scores a point, and you give student 3A a definition for which you expect a correctly spelled matching vocabulary word. Continue giving Team A definitions until some team member makes an incorrect response. An incorrect response sends the game back to the jumbled-word face off, this time with students 2A and 2B. Instead of repeating giving definitions to the first few students of each team, continue with the student after the one who gave the last incorrect response on the team. For example, if Team B wins the jumbled-word face-off, and student 5B gave the last incorrect answer for Team B, you would start this round of definition questions with student 6B, and so on. The team with the most points wins!

7. Have students write a story in which they correctly use as many vocabulary words as possible. Have students read their compositions orally! Post the most original compositions on your bulletin board!

LESSONS ELEVEN AND TWELVE

Objectives:
1. To have students practice working together in small groups
2. To encourage students' creativity
3. To encourage logical thinking

Activity

Distribute the Future Worlds Project Assignment sheet. Discuss the directions in detail and give students ample time to work in class. Be sure to tell students when their projects will be due.

LESSON THIRTEEN

Objectives
1. To widen the breadth of students' knowledge about the topics discussed or touched upon in *Fahrenheit 451*
2. To check students' nonfiction reading assignments

Activity

Ask each student to give a brief oral report about the nonfiction work he/she read for the nonfiction reading assignment. Your criteria for evaluating this report will vary depending on the level of your students. You may wish for students to give a complete report without using notes of any kind, or you may want students to read directly from a written report, or you may want to do something in between these two extremes. Just make students aware of your criteria in ample time for them to prepare their reports.

Start with one student's report. After that, ask if anyone else in the class has read on a topic related to the first student's report. If no one has, choose another student at random. After each report, be sure to ask if anyone has a report related to the one just completed. That will help keep a continuity during the discussion of the reports.

FUTURE WORLDS PROJECT - *Fahrenheit 451*

PROMPT

In Writing Assgginment #2 you gave some thought to how you think the world might be 50 years from now. Now you'll get together with a partner or two and put your ideas together to create a whole world.

Your assignment is to make a 10-15 minute presentation showing what you think our world will be like in 50 years.

REQUIREMENTS

1. Your presentation must last between 10 and 15 minutes.
2. Each member of your group must participate in the actual presentation.
3. Each member of your group must create at least one visual aid to use in your presentation.
4. Each of the topics on the Future World Worksheet must be covered in your presentation.

GETTING STARTED

As a group, decide on the answers to the questions on the Future World Worksheet. Write them down so you have them as guidelines.

Decide how you will present all of this information. Will you create a skit with some people from the future talking to each other about their world? Will you create a video as a travelogue for tourists to your world? Will you make a newspaper (copies for everyone in the class) with news stories, lifestyle articles, sports section, advertising for products, etc.? Will you write and produce a song about your times, performed by people in your world? There are lots of different, creative possibilities from which you could choose. What will you do?

After you have decided what you will do for your presentation, make a list of things that need to be done and materials that need to be gathered. Next to each item on the list, write to whom that job has been assigned. Remember, each student must create at least one visual aid to use in the presentation.

Now that your job duties are assigned, do them. You don't have a whole lot of time for this project, so you need to get the actual work done right away.

THE PRESENTATIONS

In a few days, we'll have a Future Worlds Day, during which you all will give your presentations. It should be a lot of fun as well as give us all a lot of food for thought about the future.

FUTURE WORLD WORKSHEET - *Fahrenheit 451*

In creating your world of the future, consider at least these things:

Government - What kind(s) of government(s) will there be?

Education - How will people learn?

Homes - What will people's homes look like inside and out?

Work - What kinds of jobs will there be for people to do, if any?

Economy - How will goods and services be available, and what kind of monetary system will people use?

Leisure - What leisure time activities will people have?

Family - Will society be family-oriented or otherwise structured?

Food - What will people eat, and how will it be provided & prepared?

Clothing - What will people wear?

Climate - What will the climate be?

Ecology/Environment - How will our planet look?

Other Life Forms - What other kinds of plants and animals will be sharing our planet?

Peace or War - Will the people on Earth be getting along or fighting with each other?

Space Exploration - What will the status of space exploration be?

Health - Will people be healthy? What kinds of diseases will exist, if any? What progress will medical science make in the next 50 years?

Quality of Life - What will the quality of life be on Earth in 50 years?

LESSON FOURTEEN

Objectives
1. To discuss the issue of censorship
2. To make students aware that almost everything they read and see is biased

NOTE: In many of your communities, there are debates raging about what books should be put into the library, which books should be taught in the classrooms, and/or what books should be banned from both places.

The purpose of this lesson is to make students aware of these debates. If such a thing is happening in your school district, bring in the books that are under question and explain both sides of the debate in detail to your students. In fact, you may want to arrange a debate between the arguing parties right in your classroom so students can see first-hand the arguments being made.

In addition, students should be made aware that almost everything they see/read/hear is biased. It is very rare to find anything truly objective in print these days. Include the idea, too that even the news we hear is biased: someone decides which stories to put over the air waves, and which ones will be shelved. Someone decides which stories will be printed in the newspaper and which ones will be trashed. Advertising bombards us all constantly; it is most definitely biased. The point is to make students *aware* that the media is controlled by *people*, and it is often used to directly or indirectly express the opinions *of* those people.

Activity
Pose these questions to students:

1. Are there good books and bad books? What's the difference?
2. What is the First Amendment?
3. Who decides what news will be published or broadcast? What effect does that have on what we see and hear?
4. Are there certain things that should not be published? If so, what? If not, why not?
5. Who has a right to privacy? Who has a right to know private things? What is private?
6. What is a journalist's responsibility to the public? What is a journalist's responsibility to the person being interviewed? Are there or should there be limitations placed on journalists?
7. Who has the right to decide what is good for you or me? Who gave them that power?
8. If you control the media, what do you control?
9. What would our world be like without books, magazines, newspapers, and the freedom of the press?

LESSON FIFTEEN

Objective
 To complete the Future World projects

Activity
 Have each of the groups give their presentations about the future world. If you like, you could decorate your room in a futuristic way. Maybe some of the groups will be serving foods and beverages of the future. That would be fun. Use your imagination to make it a fun, special day.

LESSON SIXTEEN

Objective
 1. To give students the opportunity to practice writing to persuade
 2. To show students how to do a comparison/contrast composition
 3. To give the teacher a chance to evaluate students' individual writing

Activity
 Distribute Writing Assignment #2. Discuss the directions orally in detail. Allow the remaining class time for students to complete the activity.

 If students do not have enough class time to finish, the papers may be collected at the beginning of the next class period.

LESSON SEVENTEEN

Objective
 To review the main ideas presented in *Fahrenheit 451*

Activity #1
 Choose one of the review games/activities included in the packet and spend your class period as outlined there. Some materials for these activities are located in the Unit Resource section of this unit.

Activity #2
 Remind students that the Unit Test will be in the next class meeting. Stress the review of the Study Guides and their class notes as a last minute, brush-up review for homework.

WRITING ASSIGNMENT #3 - *Fahrenheit 451*

PROMPT

Well, we know what it is like living in our world today. And now we have some ideas about how our future might be. Which one is better?

Your assignment is to convince me that either our world today is better than the future will be or that the future will be better than our world is today.

PREWRITING

Decide for yourself which you think will be better: the present world or the world of the future. Write down three of the most important things that convinced you to make your decision. On a piece of paper, make two columns. Title one "Now" and title the other one "Future." Down the left-hand margin of your paper, leaving plenty of space in between, write down the three most important things that convinced you to make your decision in the paragraph above. Now fill in the little chart you have made. Consider the first thing. Write down how it is today in your "Now" column. Write down how it will be in the "Future" column. Do the same thing with each of the items in your far-left column.

DRAFTING

Write a paragraph in which you introduce the idea that either today is better than the future or that the future is better than the present.

In the body of your composition, write one paragraph for each of your main points. Take your first "most important thing that convinced you" and write a paragraph about that. Make a topic sentence in which you tell your reason why the "Now" or "Future" world will be better. Fill out your paragraph by comparing our world today with the future world on this point. (Use your chart.) Write one paragraph in this way for each of your three reasons.

Write a concluding paragraph in which you summarize your ideas and conclude your composition.

PROMPT

When you finish the rough draft of your paper, ask a student who sits near you to read it. After reading your rough draft, he/she should tell you what he/she liked best about your work, which parts were difficult to understand, and ways in which your work could be improved. Reread your paper considering your critic's comments, and make the corrections you think are necessary.

PROOFREADING

Do a final proofreading of your paper double-checking your grammar, spelling, organization, and the clarity of your ideas.

1. Ask the class to make up a unit test for *Fahrenheit 451*. The test should have 4 sections: matching, true/false, short answer, and essay. Students may use 1/2 period to make the test and then swap papers and use the other 1/2 class period to take a test a classmate has devised. (open book) You may want to use the unit test included in this packet or take questions from the students' unit tests to formulate your own test.

2. Take 1/2 period for students to make up true and false questions (including the answers). Collect the papers and divide the class into two teams. Draw a big tic-tac-toe board on the chalk board. Make one team X and one team O. Ask questions to each side, giving each student one turn. If the question is answered correctly, that students' team's letter (X or O) is placed in the box. If the answer is incorrect, no mark is placed in the box. The object is to get three marks in a row like tic-tac-toe. You may want to keep track of the number of games won for each team.

3. Take 1/2 period for students to make up questions (true/false and short answer). Collect the questions. Divide the class into two teams. You'll alternate asking questions to individual members of teams A & B (like in a spelling bee). The question keeps going from A to B until it is correctly answered, then a new question is asked. A correct answer does not allow the team to get another question. Correct answers are +2 points; incorrect answers are -1 point.

4. Have students pair up and quiz each other from their study guides and class notes.

5. Give students a *Fahrenheit 451* crossword puzzle to complete.

6. Divide your class into two teams. Use the *Fahrenheit 451* crossword words with their letters jumbled as a word list. Student 1 from Team A faces off against Student 1 from Team B. You write the first jumbled word on the board. The first student (1A or 1B) to unscramble the word wins the chance for his/her team to score points. If 1A wins the jumble, go to student 2A and give him/her a clue. He/she must give you the correct word which matches that clue. If he/she does, Team A scores a point, and you give student 3A a clue for which you expect another correct response. Continue giving Team A clues until some team member makes an incorrect response. An incorrect response sends the game back to the jumbled-word face off, this time with students 2A and 2B. Instead of repeating giving clues to the first few students of each team, continue with the student after the one who gave the last incorrect response on the team. For example, if Team B wins the jumbled-word face-off, and student 5B gave the last incorrect answer for Team B, you would start this round of clue questions with student 6B, and so on. The team with the most points wins!

UNIT TESTS

This page is left blank for two-sided printing.

LESSON EIGHTEEN

Objective

To test students' understanding of the main ideas and themes in Fahrenheit 451

Activity #1

Distribute the unit tests. Go over the instructions in detail and allow students the entire class period to complete the exam.

NOTES ABOUT THE TESTS IN THIS UNIT:

There are 5 different unit tests which follow.

There are two short answer tests which are based primarily on facts from the novel.

There is one advanced short answer unit test. It is based on the extra discussion questions and quotations. Use the matching key for short answer unit test 2 to check the matching section of the advanced short answer unit test. There is no key for the short answer questions and quotations; the answers will be based on the discussions you have had during class.

There are two multiple choice unit tests. Following the two unit tests, you will find an answer sheet on which students chould mark their answers. The same answer sheet should be used for both tests; however, students' answers will be different for each test. Following the students' answer sheet for the multiple choice tests you will find your answer keys.

The short answer tests have a vocabulary section. You should choose 10 of the vocabulary words from this unit, read them orally and have the students write them down. Then, either have students write definitions or use the words in sentences.

Use these words for the vocabulary section of the advanced short answer unit test:

dictum	grotesque	imperceptibly	indecisive
melancholy	noncombustible	obscure	proclivities
receptacle	retaliation	simultaneously	tactile

Activity #2

Collect all test papers and assigned books prior to the end of the class period.

SHORT ANSWER UNIT TEST 1 - *Fahrenheit 451*

I. Matching

_____ 1. Beatty

A. Snatched books & hid them & got in trouble

_____ 2. Bradbury

B. Informer; attempted suicide

_____ 3. Clarisse

C. In charge of the local firemen

_____ 4. Faber

D. Author

_____ 5. Mildred

E. Helped Montag

_____ 6. Montag

F. Liked to think & talk, and was killed

II. Short Answer

1. How did the firemen know which houses had books?

2. What did Montag do in the old lady's attic?

3. What was Montag afraid would be discovered in his home?

4. What plan did Montag devise?

5. Why did Montag burn the book of poetry in the wall incinerator in his home?

6. Who was the informant on Montag's home?

7. Why did Montag take whiskey, a suitcase, and some of Faber's dirty clothes with him?

8. Why did the camera identify an innocent man as being Montag?

III. Composition

What is the point of *Fahrenheit 451*? When we read books, we usually come away from our reading experience a little richer, having given more thought to a particular aspect of life. What do you think Ray Bradbury intended us to gain from reading his novel?

IV. Vocabulary

Listen to the vocabulary words and write them down. Go back later and fill in the correct definition for each word.

1.

2.

3.

4.

5.

6.

7.

8.

9.

10.

SHORT ANSWER UNIT TEST 2 - *Fahrenheit 451*

I. Matching

_____ 1. Beatty   A. Helped Montag

_____ 2. Bradbury   B. Liked to think & talk, and was killed

_____ 3. Clarisse   C. Snatched books & hid them & got in trouble

_____ 4. Faber   D. Author

_____ 5. Mildred   E. In charge of the local firemen

_____ 6. Montag   F. Informer; attempted suicide

II. Short Answer

1. What are parlor-walls?

2. How did the firemen know which houses had books?

3. Why were the alarms to burn always at night?

4. Why did Captain Beatty believe books should be destroyed?

5. What three elements did Faber feel were missing from life?

6. What was different about the hobos Montag Met? Why did each man identify himself as a famous author or piece of literature?

III. Composition

1. Compare and contrast Mildred and Clarisse.

2. What kinds of things happened in the city? What kinds of things happened in the country? Why?

3. What are the main conflicts in the story? Are all the conflicts resolved at the end of the story? Explain how or why not.

4. What were the worst things about Montag's society?

5. Why didn't it matter that the authorities got the wrong man in the end?

IV. Vocabulary

Listen to the vocabulary words and write them down. Go back later and fill in the correct definition for each word.

1.

2.

3.

4.

5.

6.

7.

8.

9.

10.

KEY: SHORT ANSWER UNIT TESTS - *Fahrenheit 451*

The short answer questions are taken directly from the study guides.
If you need to look up the answers, you will find them in the study guide section.

Answers to the composition questions will vary depending on your
class discussions and the level of your students.

For the vocabulary section of the test, choose ten of the words
from the vocabulary lists to read orally for your students.

The answers to the matching section of the test are below.

Test #1	Test #2
1. C	1. E
2. D	2. D
3. F	3. B
4. E	4. A
5. B	5. F
6. A	6. C

ADVANCED SHORT ANSWER UNIT TEST - *Fahrenheit 451*

I. Short Answer

1. Compare and contrast Mildred and Clarisse.

2. What was Faber's role in the story? Why was he included?

3. What did Faber mean when he said, "I don't talk things, sir. I talk the meaning of things. I sit here and know I am alive."?

4. Why were the books banned in Montag's society?

5. "Come on, now, we're going to go build a mirror-factory first and put out nothing but mirrors for the next year and take a long look in them." Why?

6. "We're remembering. That's where we'll win out in the long run." What does that mean?

7. "I'll get hold of it so it'll never run off. I'll hold onto the world tight some day. I've got one finger on it now; that's a beginning." What does Montag mean? Why does he feel this way?

8. Why is it important to read? Why are books important to society?

9. How does Ray Bradbury make his story believable?

III. Vocabulary

Write down the vocabulary words you are given. Go back later and use all of those vocabulary words in a composition relating to *Fahrenheit 451*.

I. Multiple Choice

1. Who is Guy Montag?
   a. He is a librarian
   b. He is the mayor
   c. He is a doctor
   d. He is a fireman

2. Describe Montag's job.
   a. He maintains information files for the city.
   b. He teaches school
   c. He finds books and burns them
   d. He is a curator in a museum

3. What were parlor walls?
   a. They were a kind of surround television with which the audience could interact.
   b. They were portable partitions that could be repositioned to create a variety of living spaces.
   c. They were hidden microphones that could monitor conversations.
   d. They were barricades that separated one neighborhood from another.

4. Clarisse was part of the old society where talking and thinking were appreciated. How was this viewed by the others?
   a. She was revered as a holy one.
   b. She was thought to be insane.
   c. She was considered anti-social.
   d. She was tolerated with amusement.

5. Who was Captain Beatty?
   a. He was Montag's boss at work.
   b. He was a retired naval officer. He often told old sea stories.
   c. He was the mayor.
   d. He was Clarisse's uncle.

6. How did the firemen know which houses had books?
   a. The books all had bar codes on the back covers. These could be read for up to one mile away by a special computerized track.
   b. Neighbors, family members, and friends became informants and telephoned the authorities.
   c. They conducted random searches.
   d. The fire dogs could sniff them out.

7. What happened to Clarisse?
    a. She was hit by a car.
    b. She was hypnotized and forced to change her thinking.
    c. She was attacked by a pack of mechanical hounds.
    d. She escaped to the wilderness and joined the rebels.

8. Who was Faber?
    a. He was Montag's brother-in-law, and another sympathizer.
    b. He was second in command after Beatty.
    c. He was a retired English professor.
    d. He was the chief physician at Emergency Hospital.

9. Faber felt that three elements were missing from life. Which of these was NOT one of the elements?
    a. Quality and texture of information
    b. The satisfaction of choosing one's own job
    c. Leisure time to think
    d. The right to carry out actions based on the other two items

10. What was the destination of the alarm on the night Montag returned to work at the firehouse?
    a. The destination was the town library.
    b. The destination was Montag's home.
    c. The destination was the hospital. A few of the doctors were giving books to the patients.
    d. It was Faber's home.

11. Who was the final informant on Montag's home?
    a. It was Faber.
    b. It was Mildred.
    c. It was Beatty.
    d. It was Mrs. Phelps.

12. Why did Montag kill Captain Beatty?
    a. Montag was insane because he saw his books burning.
    b. It was an accident, Montag's finger slipped on the safety catch on the flame thrower, and Beatty got in the way.
    c. Beatty was aware that Montag was wearing a radio transmitter, and he was determined to find out who was on the other end.
    d. He wanted to stop the firemen from burning more books.

13. During the manhunt for Montag by the hound, why did the camera identify an innocent man
    as Montag?
        a. Faber deliberately misled them to get them off of Montag's trail.
        b. The computer that was tracking him malfunctioned and identified the wrong man.
        c. Nobody really knew what he looked like, so they didn't know whom to chase.
        d. The firemen needed to look good, and put a neat ending on the day's work.

14. How were these men, the hobos, preserving literature?
        a. They had built a secret fireproof library underground and quietly collected books.
        b. Each carried a backpack full of books. It was his duty to safeguard them.
        c. They were burying books in holes along the railroad tracks. They had developed a
           secret marking system so they knew where the books were.
        d. Each man had memorized a piece of literature to be written down at a later time.

II. Composition

What was wrong with Montag's world? Give a complete answer using specific examples from the book.

IV. Vocabulary

___ 1. NONCOMBUSTIBLE

A. Wordiness

___ 2. CAPILLARY

B. Predispositions; tendencies

___ 3. CENTRIFUGE

C. Deflected; avoided

___ 4. PEDANTS

D. Apparatus consisting of a compartment spun around a central axis

___ 5. JUGGERNAUT

E. Does not burn easily

___ 6. CADENCED

F. A container that holds matter

___ 7. VERBIAGE

G. Sadness; gloominess

___ 8. STOLID

H. Bizarre; distorted

___ 9. TACTILE

I. Arousing strong dislike or displeasure

___ 10. RETALIATION

J. Fine; small in diameter

___ 11. SMOLDERING

K. Burning with little smoke and no flame

___ 12. OBSCURE

L. Not readily noticed or seen; not commonly known

___ 13. IMPERCEPTIBLY

M. Returning like for like, especially evil

___ 14. MELANCHOLY

N. Authoritative pronouncement

___ 15. ODIOUS

O. Having or revealing little emotion

___ 16. RECEPTACLE

P. Impossible to detect by ordinary senses

___ 17. PROCLIVITIES

Q. With a rhythmic flow

___ 18. DICTUM

R. Those who flaunt their knowledge

___ 19. PARRIED

S. Overwhelming, advancing sight crushing all in its path

___ 20. GROTESQUE

T. Relating to the sense of touch

I. Multiple Choice

1. Who is Guy Montag?
    a. He is a librarian
    b. He is a fireman
    c. He is a doctor
    d. He is the mayor

2. Describe Montag's job.
    a. He finds books and burns them
    b. He teaches school
    c. He maintains information files for the city.
    d. He is a curator in a museum

3. What were parlor walls?
    a. They were barricades that separated one neighborhood from another.
    b. They were portable partitions that could be repositioned to create a variety of living spaces.
    c. They were hidden microphones that could monitor conversations.
    d. They were a kind of surround television with which the audience could interact.

4. Clarisse was part of the old society where talking and thinking were appreciated. How was this viewed by the others?
    a. She was revered as a holy one.
    b. She was thought to be insane.
    c. She was tolerated with amusement.
    d. She was considered anti-social.

5. Who was Captain Beatty?
    a. He was a retired naval officer. He often told old sea stories.
    b. He was Montag's boss at work.
    c. He was the mayor.
    d. He was Clarisse's uncle.

6. How did the firemen know which houses had books?
    a. Neighbors, family members, and friends became informants and telephoned the authorities.
    b. The books all had bar codes on the back covers. These could be read for up to one mile away by a special computerized track.
    c. They conducted random searches.
    d. The fire dogs could sniff them out.

7. What happened to Clarisse?
    a. She was hypnotized and forced to change her thinking.
    b. She was hit by a car.
    c. She was attacked by a pack of mechanical hounds.
    d. She escaped to the wilderness and joined the rebels.

8. Who was Faber?
    a. He was Montag's brother-in-law, and another sympathizer.
    b. He was second in command after Beatty.
    c. He was the chief physician at Emergency Hospital.
    d. He was a retired English professor.

9. Faber felt that three elements were missing from life. Which of these was NOT one of the elements?
    a. Quality and texture of information
    b. Leisure time to think
    c. The satisfaction of choosing one's own job
    d. The right to carry out actions based on the other two items

10. What was the destination of the alarm on the night Montag returned to work at the firehouse?
    a. The destination was Montag's home.
    b. The destination was the town library.
    c. The destination was the hospital. A few of the doctors were giving books to the patients.
    d. It was Faber's home.

11. Who was the final informant on Montag's home?
    a. It was Mildred.
    b. It was Faber.
    c. It was Beatty.
    d. It was Mrs. Phelps.

12. Why did Montag kill Captain Beatty?
    a. Montag was insane because he saw his books burning.
    b. Beatty was aware that Montag was wearing a radio transmitter, and he was determined to find out who was on the other end.
    c. It was an accident, Montag's finger slipped on the safety catch on the flame thrower, and Beatty got in the way.
    d. He wanted to stop the firemen from burning more books.

13. During the manhunt for Montag by the hound, why did the camera identify an innocent man as Montag?
      a. Faber deliberately misled them to get them off of Montag's trail.
      b. The computer that was tracking him malfunctioned and identified the wrong man.
      c. Nobody really knew what he looked like, so they didn't know whom to chase.
      d. The firemen needed to look good, and put a neat ending on the day's work.

14. How were these men, the hobos, preserving literature?
      a. They had built a secret fireproof library underground and quietly collected books.
      b. Each man had memorized a piece of literature to be written down at a later time.
      c. They were burying books in holes along the railroad tracks. They had developed a secret marking system so they knew where the books were.
      d. Each carried a backpack full of books. It was his duty to safeguard them.

II. Composition

The *New York Times* said, "Frightening in its implications, Mr. Bradbury's account of this insane world, which bears many alarming resemblances to our own, is fascinating." What are the "frightening implications," and what "alarming resemblances" does Montag's world have to our own?

III. Vocabulary

___ 1. RECEPTACLE   A. With a rhythmic flow

___ 2. NONCOMBUSTIBLE   B. Apparatus consisting of a compartment spun around
                                           a central axis

___ 3. PRATFALL   C. Wordiness

___ 4. CAPILLARY   D. Overwhelming, advancing sight crushing all in its path

___ 5. COWARDICE   E. Arousing strong dislike or displeasure

___ 6. RAVENOUS   F. Not able to make a decision

___ 7. RETALIATION   G. Deflected; avoided

___ 8. PARRIED   H. Humiliating failure; a fall on the buttocks

___ 9. MELANCHOLY   I. Extremely hungry; greedy for gratification

___ 10. CADENCED   J. The study of the dynamics of projectiles

___ 11. VERBIAGE   K. Ignoble fear in the face of danger

___ 12. JUGGERNAUT   L. Not readily noticed or seen; not commonly known

___ 13. CENTRIFUGE   M. Bizarre; distorted

___ 14. ODIOUS   N. Returning like for like, especially evil

___ 15. GROTESQUE   O. Having many faces

___ 16. INDECISIVE   P. Those who flaunt their knowledge

___ 17. BALLISTICS   Q. Sadness; gloominess

___ 18. OBSCURE   R. Fine; small in diameter

___ 19. PEDANTS   S. Does not burn easily

___ 20. MULTIFACETED   T. A container that holds matter

ANSWER SHEET - *Fahrenheit 451*
Multiple Choice Unit Tests

I. Multiple Choice

1. ___
2. ___
3. ___
4. ___
5. ___
6. ___
7. ___
8. ___
9. ___
10. ___
11. ___
12. ___
13. ___
14. ___

III. Vocabulary

1. ___   11. ___
2. ___   12. ___
3. ___   13. ___
4. ___   14. ___
5. ___   15. ___
6. ___   16. ___
7. ___   17. ___
8. ___   18. ___
9. ___   19. ___
10. ___   20. ___

II. Composition Use the space below and the back of this page for your composition.

ANSWER KEY MULTIPLE CHOICE UNIT TESTS -- *Fahrenheit 451*

Answers to Test 1 are in the left hand column. Answers to Test 2 are in the right hand column.

I. Multiple Choice

1. D B
2. C A
3. A D
4. C D
5. A B
6. B A
7. A B
8. C D
9. B C
10. B A
11. B A
12. C B
13. D D
14. D B

III. Vocabulary

1. E T   11. K C
2. J S   12. L D
3. D H   13. P B
4. R R   14. G E
5. S K   15. I M
6. Q I   16. F F
7. A N   17. B J
8. O G   18. N L
9. T Q   19. C P
10. M A   20. H O

This page is left blank for two-sided printing.

UNIT RESOURCE MATERIALS

This page is left blank for two-sided printing.

BULLETIN BOARD IDEAS - *Fahrenheit 451*

1. Save one corner of the board for the best of students' *Fahrenheit 451* writing assignments.

2. Take one of the word search puzzles from the extra activities packet and with a marker copy it over in a large size on the bulletin board. Write the clue words to find to one side. Invite students prior to and after class to find the words and circle them on the bulletin board.

3. Write several of the most significant quotations from the book onto the board on brightly colored paper.

4. Make a bulletin board listing the vocabulary words for this unit. As you complete sections of the novel and discuss the vocabulary for each section, write the definitions on the bulletin board. (If your board is one students face frequently, it will help them learn the words.)

5. Title the board "IN THE YEAR 2525" and post the lyrics to this popular 1970's tune. Find pictures which relate to the lyrics. Take time to discuss the ideas presented by the song with your students.

6. Do a bulletin board about censorship, free speech, and the First Amendment.

7. Draw a big red thermometer with the red going up to 451 degrees Fahrenheit. Next to it, draw a big fire and have book covers appear to be going into it.

8. Do a bulletin board about fire prevention.

9. Make a bulletin board promoting reading. Make a title "PICK UP A BOOK OR MAGA-ZINE AND READ! YOUR BRAIN WILL THANK YOU!" or "EXERCISE YOUR BRAIN: READ!" Post book jackets of books you think your students would enjoy, magazine covers, anything with printed material.

10. Do a bulletin board about the future of our planet, promoting recycling, conservation, responsible use of our resources, etc.

11. Title the board: WORKING FOR A BETTER TOMORROW. Post pictures of people doing things that are obviously intended to make our world a better place in which to live.

12. Title the board: MAKING OUR WORLD A BETTER PLACE. Have each student write up on the board something he/she can do (will do, should do) to make his/her neighborhood a better place to live.

EXTRA ACTIVITIES - *Fahrenheit 451*

One of the difficulties in teaching a novel is that all students don't read at the same speed. One student who likes to read may take the book home and finish it in a day or two. Sometimes a few students finish the in-class assignments early. The problem, then, is finding suitable extra activities for students.

The best thing I've found is to keep a little library in the classroom. For this unit on *Fahrenheit 451*, you might check out from the school library other books and articles by Ray Bradbury. A biography or articles about the author or criticisms of the book would be interesting for some students. You can include other related books and articles about censorship, reading, firemen, technological inventions, leisure-time activities, television (and its effect on us!), news broadcasts, or ecology.

Other things you may keep on hand are puzzles. We have made some relating directly to *Fahrenheit 451* for you. Feel free to duplicate them.

Some students may like to draw. You might devise a contest or allow some extra-credit grade for students who draw characters or scenes from *Fahrenheit 451*. Note, too, that if the students do not want to keep their drawings you may pick up some extra bulletin board materials this way. If you have a contest and you supply the prize (a CD or something like that perhaps), you could, possibly, make the drawing itself a non-returnable entry fee.

The pages which follow contain games, puzzles and worksheets. The keys, when appropriate, immediately follow the puzzle or worksheet. There are two main groups of activities: one group for the unit; that is, generally relating to the *Fahrenheit 451* text, and another group of activities related strictly to the *Fahrenheit 451* vocabulary.

Directions for these games, puzzles and worksheets are self-explanatory. The object here is to provide you with extra materials you may use in any way you choose.

MORE ACTIVITIES - *Fahrenheit 451*

1. Pick a chapter or scene with a great deal of dialogue and have the students act it out on a stage. (Perhaps you could assign various scenes to different groups of students so more than one scene could be acted and more students could participate.)

2. Use some of the related topics noted earlier as suggestions for an in-class library, as topics for research, reports, written papers, or topics for guest speakers.

3. Research what careers are currently available in journalism, fire prevention, library science, and technological sciences.

4. Have students design a book cover (front and back and inside flaps) for *Fahrenheit 451*.

5. Have students design a bulletin board (ready to be put up; not just sketched) for *Fahrenheit 451*.

6. Discuss advertising in detail. have students bring in examples of advertising. Discuss the things the ads have in common (how they are supposed to appeal to us) and what kinds of things people should beware of when they are reading advertising.

7. Have students plan and carry out a project which will improve your school or their neighborhoods.

8. Have a mini anti-drug unit. Spend some time getting your kids involved in the "Just Say No!" or some similar program. Provide information and help.

9. Discuss the effect of a society's use of drugs on that society. What do drugs do not only to the individual, but to society as a whole?

10. Discuss ways in which your community can combat drugs. What things have been done, what things are planned to be done, and what else can be done?

11. Have a read-a-thon during which students get pledges for every fifteen minutes (or however long) they read. Have students come in on a Saturday (or set aside two or three class periods) where students' time can be monitored and officially counted. Use the proceeds for your class's favorite charity or to buy more books for your English Department or library.

WORD SEARCH - *Fahrenheit 451*

All words in this list are associated with *Fahrenheit 451*. The words are placed backwards, forward, diagonally, up and down. The included words are listed below the word searches.

```
N V T B S D Q V K X H R B Z K F V J X D F G M V
Q T H R G Y C R N B N M E X Z E L R M S C H S W
D I E A T T A C K H O B O S T N A M R O F N I M
T A F S G P F S G B C O I F C C F R S I N H M Y
D Q R E S C V Y H F K U K R Y A Q R R K W T B Z
F J N X E I F S L E O N K S O K P E E Y C P A N
R I V E R N R T E L S N I G H T M E R E B A F G
W R R L Z E E A T L A L W L R E A I F A Y W R D
D X M E T M L S L P T C L W N I N R L P D A J T
S L B I L X H E O C H E I I T Y L N E D Q I R C
S H N E C Y H O G R R O E N P Q N L I N R V O D
R G H I A S C G U R E V E B A R W G E V I E F M
I R T W A T L L Z N P K C N V H E B B D C C D Q
F T P E Y X T X N N D J R J I S C Z P Z F T N P
A K S G L R L Y L J K U Q F T X J E J W V F N I
B R A D B U R Y Q L B W Y W W Y B S M B S Z R T
C A C O P H O N Y T J P J M H L N H G L J N J V
```

ASHES	CLARISSE	HOBOS	PHOENIX
ATTACK	DIE	HOUND	PILLS
ATTIC	DIGEST	IGNITER	RADIO
BEATTY	EAR	INCINERATOR	READ
BEETLES	ESCAPE	INFORMANTS	RIVER
BOMB	FABER	KEROSENE	SEASHELLS
BOOKS	FIRE	MECHANICAL	ST LOUIS
BRADBURY	FIREMEN	MILDRED	TRACKS
BURN	FREE	MONTAG	WINE
CACOPHONY	GRILLE	NIGHT	YARD
CAR	HELMET	PARK	

CROSSWORD 1 - *Fahrenheit 451*

CROSSWORD CLUES - *Fahrenheit 451*

ACROSS

1. Mildred's pastime; huge television
5. Flames
8. Opposite of out
9. Montag's path to safety
12. Clarisse was hit & killed by one
13. Mechanical ___; chased criminals
14. Opposite of in
15. Small communications device used by Montag & Faber
17. Place where radio transmitter was put for use
18. He helped Montag
20. Look with your eyes
21. Where Montag went after fleeing Faber's house
22. Mildred took an overdose of sleeping ___.
23. City car service
25. Destroy with flames
26. Inquire
27. He snatched books & hid them & got in trouble
29. What an angry dog does with his teeth
30. To get away
32. At this moment
33. Clarisse's condition after being hit by a car
34. Montag was afraid the hounds would do this
36. Montag & Faber were going to plant these in firemen's houses
37. Condensed version of a book
42. Aids
44. Fireman's head protector
45. Montag burned a book of poetry in one.
49. Transportation
50. ____ Hound
51. Time when most fires were set
55. Unusual; different
56. ____ 451

DOWN

1. Place where Montag met Faber
2. Rain tasted like this beverage
3. Coordinating conjunction
4. Faber's destination
6. People who told fireman who had books
7. Book Montag memorized
10. Montag took a book from the old lady's ___.
11. It smelled like perfume to Montag
12. She liked to think and talk
13. They memorized literature.
16. Stop living
18. They burned books & started fires
19. Wife; informer; attempted suicide
24. Montag hid his books there after the ladies left.
25. Captain of the firemen
28. Not used; not old; perhaps improved
29. One blew up the city
31. Place Montag first hid his books
34. Remains after burning
35. Harsh-sounding words
38. Sight organs
39. Flame starter
40. What an author does
41. Rising from the ashes
43. To teach someone; make more learned
46. Present plural of 'to be'
47. What we do with books
48. Stopped; finished
52. Opposite of stop
53. Also
54. They cooked bacon in it

CROSSWORD 1ANSWER KEY - *Fahrenheit 451*

		P	A	R	L	O	R	W	A	L	L	S						F	I	R	E
		A					I	N			T	RACKS					N		C		
	CAR				HOUND					L	T		E				F		C		
	L	K		O			E			O	U	T		R	A	D	I	O		L	
EAR			F	ABER			M		U		I		O		I		R		E		
	R		I	O			I	I		C		S	E	E		M		S			
RIVER				S		PIL	L		L	S			E			T	AXI			
	S		E		Y		D		B	U	R	N				N		A			
ASK		M	ON	T	AG		R		E		E		BIT		ES					
E		E	E	R		ESCAPE						O		S		T					
	G	N	OW		D	EAD			T			M				E					
	R						A	T	T	A	C	K		B	O	O	K	S			
DIGEST				I	W		S	Y	A												
P	L	Y		G	R	H			C		H	ELPS									
HEL	M	E	T	I	NCI	NERAT			O	R		D									
O	E	S	R	I	T	S	R	P	E	U											
E		BEETL		ES		M	ECH	ANI		C	AL										
NIGHT	A	E	S	F		O	D	A													
I	O	ODD	R	F	A	HRENHEI			T												
X		O		N		Y	D	E													

101

___ 1. MECHANICAL   A. Mechanical ___; chased criminals

___ 2. CACOPHONY   B. Flame starter

___ 3. ATTIC   C. Montag burned a book of poetry in one.

___ 4. ASHES   D. ___ Hound

___ 5. ATTACK   E. Harsh-sounding words

___ 6. HOUND   F. Rising from the ashes

___ 7. INFORMANTS   G. Transportation

___ 8. INCINERATOR   H. Fireman's head protector

___ 9. WINE   I. She liked to think and talk

___ 10. BURN   J. People who told fireman who had books

___ 11. KEROSENE   K. Destroy with flames

___ 12. PARLORWALLS   L. Mildred's pastime; huge television

___ 13. PHOENIX   M. Time when most fires were set

___ 14. BEETLES   N. Remains after burning

___ 15. RADIO   O. It smelled like perfume to Montag

___ 16. IGNITER   P. Rain tasted like this beverage

___ 17. HELMET   Q. Montag took a book from the old lady's ___.

___ 18. NIGHT   R. Small communications device used by Montag & Faber

___ 19. PILLS   S. Montag was afraid the hounds would do this

___ 20. CLARISSE   T. Mildred took an overdose of sleeping ___.

MATCHING QUIZ/WORKSHEET 2 - *Fahrenheit 451*

___ 1. FIRE   A. Ear thimbles

___ 2. ASHES   B. Remains after burning

___ 3. GRILLE   C. She liked to think and talk

___ 4. CLARISSE   D. Not bound

___ 5. IGNITER   E. Montag & Faber were going to plant these in firemen's houses

___ 6. SEASHELLS   F. He helped Montag

___ 7. BURN   G. Montag hid his books there after the ladies left.

___ 8. ATTIC   H. Place where radio transmitter was put for use

___ 9. FIREMEN   I. Place Montag first hid his books

___ 10. CAR   J. Clarisse was hit & killed by one

___ 11. INFORMANTS   K. They burned books & started fires

___ 12. INCINERATOR   L. Destroy with flames

___ 13. FABER   M. Montag burned a book of poetry in one.

___ 14. FREE   N. People who told fireman who had books

___ 15. BOOKS   O. Rising from the ashes

___ 16. EAR   P. Place where Montag met Faber

___ 17. YARD   Q. Harsh-sounding words

___ 18. PARK   R. Montag took a book from the old lady's ___.

___ 19. PHOENIX   S. Flame starter

___ 20. CACOPHONY   T. Flames

Worksheet 1	Worksheet 2
1. D	1. T
2. E	2. B
3. Q	3. I
4. N	4. C
5. S	5. S
6. A	6. A
7. J	7. L
8. C	8. R
9. P	9. K
10. K	10. J
11. O	11. N
12. L	12. M
13. F	13. F
14. G	14. D
15. R	15. E
16. B	16. H
17. H	17. G
18. M	18. P
19. T	19. O
20. I	20. Q

JUGGLE LETTER REVIEW GAME CLUE SHEET - *Fahrenheit 451*

SCRAMBLED	WORD	CLUE
CPAESE	ESCAPE	To get away
EADR	READ	What we do with books
OBKSO	BOOKS	Montag & Faber were going to plant these in firemen's houses
RPKA	PARK	Place where Montag met Faber
TDESGI	DIGEST	Condensed version of a book
CHYNCPOAO	CACOPHONY	Harsh-sounding words
ARIOD	RADIO	Communications device used by Montag and Faber
TITCA	ATTIC	Montag took a book from the old lady's _____
NEEMIFR	FIREMEN	They burned books & started fires
OESEEKRN	KEROSENE	It smelled like perfume to Montag
OHOSB	HOBOS	They memorized literature
THFAREHINE	FAHRENHEIT	_____ 451
IED	DIE	Stop living
UYDRARBB	BRADBURY	Author
LROLLPSWAAR	PARLORWALLS	Mildred's pastime; huge television
NRUB	BURN	Destroy with flames
HEXOINP	PHOENIX	Rising from the ashes
RDAY	YARD	Montag hid his books there after the ladies left
ELGIRL	GRILLE	Place Montag first hid his books
ASCKTR	TRACKS	Montag's path to safety
EIRNANTRICO	INCINERATOR	Montag burned a book of poetry in one
FMTAISNNRO	INFORMANTS	People who told fireman who had books
VRRIE	RIVER	Where Montag went after fleeing Faber's house
IEAEETSCLCSS	ECCLESIASTES	Book Montag memorized
NAMICALECH	MECHANICAL	_____Hound
ISLCERSA	CLARISSE	She like to think and talk
ETMELH	HELMET	Fireman's head protector
RCA	CAR	Clarisse was hit and killed by one
LSISTOU	ST LOUIS	Faber's destination
EASSH	ASHES	Remains after burning
AYBTTE	BEATTY	Captain of the firemen
EEFR	FREE	Not bound
ELBEEST	BEETLES	Transportation
THNIG	NIGHT	Time when most fires were set
RVIRE	RIVER	Where Montag went after fleeing Faber's house
BFRAE	FABER	He helped Montag
IEFR	FIRE	Flames
MBBO	BOMB	One blew up the city
ETIRNGI	IGNITER	Flame starter

This page is left blank for two-sided printing.

VOCABULARY RESOURCE MATERIALS

This page is left blank for two-sided printing.

VOCABULARY WORD SEARCH - *Fahrenheit 451*

All words in this list are associated with *Fahrenheit 451* with an emphasis on the vocabulary words chosen for study in the text. The words are placed backwards, forward, diagonally, up and down. The included words are listed below.

```
C N N V C S M B Q L J Z J M H S W L G N Y T V D
D R N M T X P P C L B N H M V H L K L S B K F W
X W X O G N C U Y H X R T P A A N D U Z Z F S W
L T L D N N N D L R Y D H B F N T O E V S U T E
T I N D E C I S I V E R E T A L I A T I O N R V
D H M S E C O R V T E G A C U D C F C N R U J S
H S J N T T E M E H I R A L O A R A E T C R G H
G X E U E C C B D P M I I L T N V R S I V A S
S R M I F D A A I U L R P Z B I A R B D T L P P
W N O J T F V D R D S O E E E R P O E J A E E D
H M V T I I T H E F R T M C R D E A B G Y M D B
S R E T E W V S N N E A I S E C E V C Y G G O L
B A L L I S T I C S C R W B T P E T S S L U Q N
R U R N A N Q Y L R B E T O L K T P C Z Z B J D
M V C H A N P U P C Q V D G C E H A T E F G Q N
S Q B D L B C R E R O W F F C J M M C I R Y X D
W S E X L T C H K P L R N S S K Z R N L B E B W
T P T G R B F L O H D R P T G W K L X M E L W T
N J W S Y P M M T L N C P Z F K C D X X B L Y G
C E N T R I F U G E Y L S U O E N A T L U M I S
```

BALLISTICS	IMPERCEPTIBLY	ODIOUS	REFRACTED
CADENCED	INDECISIVE	PARRIED	RETALIATION
CAPILLARY	JUGGERNAUT	PEDANTS	SMOLDERING
CARDAMON	LIMNED	PRATFALL	STOLID
CENTRIFUGE	MANIFESTED	PROCLIVITIES	TACTILE
COWARDICE	MELANCHOLY	PULVERIZED	VERBIAGE
DICTUM	MULTIFACETED	PYRE	
ERECTED	NONCOMBUSTIBLE	RAVENOUS	
GROTESQUE	OBSCURE	RECEPTACLE	
	SIMULTANEOUSLY		

VOCABULARY CROSSWORD CLUES - *Fahrenheit 451*

ACROSS

1. Deflected from a straight path
7. Montag took a book from the old lady's ___.

9. A pile of combustible materials for burning a corpse
10. Montag & Faber were going to plant these in firemen's houses
11. Fine; small in diameter
13. Skepticism; disbelief; question the truth of
14. Definite article
15. Described
16. Distress signal
17. Stop living
18. Sadness; gloominess
21. He helped Montag
24. Where Montag went after fleeing Faber's house
25. Impossible to detect by ordinary senses
29. Angry or crazy
30. Unbelievably strange; far-fetched
31. Place Montag first hid his books
33. Grab away from; snatch
34. Montag was not in a car; he was on ----
35. Authoritative pronouncement
38. Relating to the sense of touch
39. Those who flaunt their knowledge
41. Clarisse was hit & killed by one
42. Arousing strong dislike or displeasure
43. Fireman's head protector
46. Having or revealing little emotion
47. Montag's path to safety

DOWN

2. Set up; established
3. Mildred picked up the phone to --- the authorities
4. To get away
5. Faber's destination
6. He snatched books & hid them & got in trouble
7. Remains after burning
8. She liked to think and talk
9. Predispositions; tendencies
10. Captain of the firemen
12. Reduced to powder
19. Indian spice
20. Returning like for like, especially evil
22. One blew up the city
23. Small communications device used by Montag & Faber
26. Humiliating failure; a fall on the buttocks
27. Deflected; avoided
28. The study of the dynamics of projectiles
32. Mechanical ___; chased criminals
36. They memorized literature.
37. Past tense of 'to eat'
39. Mildred took an overdose of sleeping ___.

40. Montag hid his books there after the ladies left.
44. Place where radio transmitter was put for use
45. Pronoun for a thing

VOCABULARY CROSSWORD ANSWER KEY - *Fahrenheit 451*

			R	E	F	R	A	C	T	E	D								S		
			R			A		S					M		A	T	T	I	C		
	PYRE					L		C			BOO		KS			L		L			
	R		C	APIL			L	ARY			E		N		H		O		A		
DOUBT				U				P			A		T	HE		U		R			
	C		E	L	I	M	N	E	D		T		A		S		I		I		
	L		D	V							T		G			S	O	S			
DIE				M	E	L	A	NCHOL			Y							S			
	V		R		R			A							F	ABER					
RIVER	I			I	M	PERC		EPTI		BLY					O		A				
	T		T		Z	R		D		A			A			M	A	D			
BIZARRE				E		A		A		G	R	I	L	L	E		H		B	I	
	E		L		D		T		M		R		L		O			O			
	S	E	I	Z	E		F	O	O	T		I		D	I	C	T	U	M		
H		A		A		A	N		E		S		N								
O		T	ACT		I	L	E		PEDANT			S		D		Y					
B	I		E		L		I			I			C	A	R						
O	DIO	US			HEL		MET		C					R							
S		N		I			L	A		S	T	O	L	I	D						
			T	R	ACKS		R														

___ 1. Authoritative pronouncement
      a. Stolid   b. Capillary   c. Parried   d. Dictum

___ 2. Those who flaunt their knowledge
      a. Simultaneously   b. Dictum   c. Pedants   d. Verbiage

___ 3. Relating to the sense of touch
      a. Tactile   b. Imperceptibly   c. Smoldering   d. Pratfall

___ 4. Not readily noticed or seen; not commonly known
      a. Juggernaut   b. Noncombustible   c. Proclivities   d. Obscure

___ 5. Deflected; avoided
      a. Indecisive   b. Refracted   c. Parried   d. Juggernaut

___ 6. The study of the dynamics of projectiles
      a. Ballistics   b. Noncombustible   c. Dictum   d. Simultaneously

___ 7. Returning like for like, especially evil
      a. Simultaneously   b. Retaliation   c. Pratfall   d. Proclivities

___ 8. Set up; established
      a. Noncombustible   b. Ravenous   c. Erected   d. Retaliation

___ 9. Does not burn easily
      a. Melancholy   b. Noncombustible   c. Pulverized   d. Juggernaut

___ 10. Extremely hungry; greedy for gratification
      a. Smoldering   b. Ravenous   c. Limned   d. Manifested

___ 11. Having or revealing little emotion
      a. Pulverized   b. Stolid   c. Retaliation   d. Ravenous

___ 12. Overwhelming, advancing sight crushing all in its path
      a. Juggernaut   b. Simultaneously   c. Pedants   d. Proclivities

___ 13. Not able to make a decision
      a. Verbiage   b. Indecisive   c. Parried   d. Pulverized

___ 14. Bizarre; distorted
      a. Centrifuge   b. Proclivities   c. Grotesque   d. Cowardice

___ 15. A container that holds matter
      a. Receptacle   b. Grotesque   c. Obscure   d. Cardamon

___ 16. Happening at the same time
      a. Multifaceted   b. Cowardice   c. Limned   d. Simultaneously

___ 17. Arousing strong dislike or displeasure
      a. Proclivities   b. Pulverized   c. Pratfall   d. Odious

___ 18. Fine; small in diameter
      a. Capillary   b. Pyre   c. Erected   d. Ballistics

___ 19. Showed; revealed
      a. Verbiage   b. Indecisive   c. Manifested   d. Ballistics

___ 20. Wordiness
      a. Stolid   b. Erected   c. Multifaceted   d. Verbiage

___ 1. NONCOMBUSTIBLE   A. Wordiness

___ 2. CAPILLARY   B. Predispositions; tendencies

___ 3. CENTRIFUGE   C. Deflected; avoided

___ 4. PEDANTS   D. Apparatus consisting of a compartment spun around a central axis

___ 5. JUGGERNAUT   E. Does not burn easily

___ 6. CADENCED   F. A container that holds matter

___ 7. VERBIAGE   G. Sadness; gloominess

___ 8. STOLID   H. Bizarre; distorted

___ 9. TACTILE   I. Arousing strong dislike or displeasure

___ 10. RETALIATION   J. Fine; small in diameter

___ 11. SMOLDERING   K. Burning with little smoke and no flame

___ 12. OBSCURE   L. Not readily noticed or seen; not commonly known

___ 13. IMPERCEPTIBLY   M. Returning like for like, especially evil

___ 14. MELANCHOLY   N. Authoritative pronouncement

___ 15. ODIOUS   O. Having or revealing little emotion

___ 16. RECEPTACLE   P. Impossible to detect by ordinary senses

___ 17. PROCLIVITIES   Q. With a rhythmic flow

___ 18. DICTUM   R. Those who flaunt their knowledge

___ 19. PARRIED   S. Overwhelming, advancing sight crushing all in its path

___ 20. GROTESQUE   T. Relating to the sense of touch

KEY: VOCABULARY WORKSHEETS - *Fahrenheit 451*

Worksheet 1	Worksheet 2
1. D	1. E
2. C	2. J
3. A	3. D
4. D	4. R
5. C	5. S
6. A	6. Q
7. B	7. A
8. C	8. O
9. B	9. T
10. B	10. M
11. B	11. K
12. A	12. L
13. B	13. P
14. C	14. G
15. A	15. I
16. D	16. F
17. D	17. B
18. A	18. N
19. C	19. C
20. D	20. H

VOCABULARY JUGGLE LETTER REVIEW GAME CLUES - *Fahrenheit 451*

SCRAMBLED	WORD	CLUE
RLCAPYLAI	CAPILLARY	Fine; small in diameter
RSUBOEC	OBSCURE	Not readily noticed or seen; not commonly known
IISIVENCED	INDECISIVE	Not able to make a decision
IRENLTTIAAO	RETALIATION	Returning like for like, especially evil
DPTNSEA	PEDANTS	Those who flaunt their knowledge
RPEY	PYRE	A pile of combustible materials for burning a corpse
LLPAARTF	PRATFALL	Humiliating failure; a fall on the buttocks
DSOUOI	ODIOUS	Arousing strong dislike or displeasure
ERTECFDAR	REFRACTED	Deflected from a straight path
DAOCANMR	CARDAMON	Indian Spice
CONYEHLAML	MELANCHOLY	Sadness; gloominess
IIPLSERVCTOI	PROCLIVITIES	Predispositions; tendencies
DFULEEITTCAM	MULTIFACETED	Having many faces
ERAVBGEI	VERBIAGE	Wordiness
DMIENL	LIMNED	Described
AGURNGUJTE	JUGGERNAUT	Overwhelming, advancing sight crushing all in its path
CEIRDOACW	COWARDICE	Ignoble fear in the face of danger
ALLSCSIIBT	BALLISTICS	The study of the dynamics of projectiles
OIDTSL	STOLID	Having or revealing little emotion
MDLORIESGN	SMOLDERING	Burning with little smoke and no flame
TRELECCAPE	RECEPTACLE	A container that holds matter
ETEDCRE	ERECTED	Set up; established
ECILTTA	TACTILE	Relating to the sense of touch
RUEEOQSTG	GROTESQUE	Bizarre; distorted
SDMEEIANTF	MANIFESTED	Showed; revealed
ZRULIEPDVE	PULVERIZED	Reduced to powder
EDDNCECA	CADENCED	With a rhythmic flow
EDPRRIA	PARRIED	Deflected; avoided
IEYLBMICPREPT	IMPERCEPTIBLY	Impossible to detect by ordinary senses
RAEFCDRTE	REFRACTED	Deflected from a straight path

CPSIA information can be obtained
at www.ICGtesting.com
Printed in the USA
BVOW10s1706050917

493950BV00002B/7/P